# IF LIFE is a GAME... THESE are the STORIES

# Other Books by Chérie Carter-Scott

# IF LIFE is a GAME...
# THESE are the STORIES

## True Stories by Real People Around the World About Being Human

◆

CHÉRIE CARTER-SCOTT Ph.D.

International Best-selling Author of

*If Life Is a Game...These Are the Rules*

**Andrews McMeel
Publishing**

Kansas City

04 05 06 07 08 RR2 10 9 8 7 6 5 4 3 2

Library of Congress Cataloging-in-Publication Data

If life is a game—these are the stories : true stories by real people around the world about being human / [compiled by] Chérie Carter-Scott.
    p. cm.
  ISBN 0-7407-4684-7
    1. Conduct of life.  I. Carter-Scott, Chérie.

BJ1597.I3 2004
128—dc22

2004043761

Book design by Tolman Creek Design

This book is dedicated to all people throughout the world who believe it is possible to live together in peace on this planet. Respect is the key that can help us transcend our differences and live in harmony. As we hold the vision, believe in the dream, and walk our talk, we will eventually evolve into peaceful people. It may take time, but it is possible, and we can never give up hope!

# CONTENTS

## RULE EIGHT
### WHAT YOU MAKE OF YOUR LIFE IS UP TO YOU                          171

## RULE NINE
### ALL YOUR ANSWERS LIE INSIDE OF YOU                               191

## RULE TEN
### YOU WILL FORGET ALL OF THIS AT BIRTH

# ACKNOWLEDGMENTS

The contributors to this book have waited patiently, believed in the process, and been willing to support it through the twists and turns in the road. They really get the credit for trusting me with their precious stories and sharing them with the world. I also wish to thank:

Elizabeth Pomada and Mike Larsen, my agents who believe in and love this book.

Jean Lucas, my editor, who sees the vision and values the mission.

Courtney Moilanen for all her marketing efforts.

To Jack Canfield, Patty Aubery, and the entire Chicken Soup for the Soul family, who started me on the journey of this book ten years ago.

Lynn Stewart, my sister and business partner for thirty years who continues to be the "wind beneath my wings." Her support is unsurpassed.

Michael Pomije, my beloved soul mate and partner who supports my visions, dreams, and goals every day of his life.

Jennifer Carter-Scott, my daughter, who has believed in and supported this dream becoming reality.

All of those who have dedicated their time, efforts, and energy to this project, including: Leah Nichols, Rachel Goldberg, Danielle Aberle, Ueli and Trix Egger, Jilian Dowling, Connie Fueyo, Elizabeth Keedy, Katrina

Goddard, Renee Noel, John Sheehan, Hedy Tillmans, Roy Martina, Patricia Martina, Norisca Rodriguez, and Barbara Del Monico. And finally, Leah Simpson, who relentlessly supported the completion of this book above and beyond the call of duty.

# RULE **1** ONE

## YOU WILL RECEIVE A BODY

*You may love it or hate it, but it will be yours for
the duration of your life on Earth.*

———◆◈◆———

L ife has its challenges—for each of us. They say you never get more tests than you can handle; however, each one of us has a different tolerance for stress. It takes incredible willpower to make the seemingly impossible happen when your options are extremely limited.

## Where There Is a Will . . . There Is Always Some Way

France

◦ ◦

*To achieve great things we must live as if we were never going to die.*

**Vauvenargues**

Jean-Dominique Bauby lived with his wife, Sylvie, his eleven-year-old son, Theophile, and his nine-year-old daughter, Celeste, in a suburb of Paris. As the chief editor of *Elle* magazine, his life was demanding. Between his family, his job, his travels, his hobbies, and his sports, he barely had time to fit everything in.

On a gray December day in 1995, Bauby was driving on an icy freeway when, without any warning, he suffered a massive stroke. He managed to stop his car and send Theophile for help before he collapsed in the backseat.

Three weeks passed before he regained consciousness from his coma. Upon awakening, he found himself drastically different from the healthy, robust man who had been driving his car to Paris. The stroke had severely impacted him; he was unable to speak or move—his entire body was paralyzed.  He noticed that he could control only the movement of his left eyelid.  Fortunately, his brain and his memory were intact and functioning perfectly.

Determined to find a way to communicate, Bauby set out to write an entire book by dictating with his left eyelid.  *Le Scaphandre et le Papillon (The Diving Suit and the Butterfly),* is a poetic and imaginative voyage through the mind of a man whose thoughts are trapped in a paralyzed body.  He wrote, "When the diving suit becomes less oppressive, the mind can flit about like a butterfly."

Bauby met with Claude Mendible for three-hour daily sessions in his hospital room as he blinked out his text, letter by letter, using a special alphabet designed for the blinking of one solitary eyelid. The 137-page text is the result of over 200,000 blinks. His keen literary mind turned him into a cosmic traveler, whirling through time and space. While nurses and aides exercised his inert limbs, childhood memories, fiction, and unfulfilled fantasies danced in his head. The legacy he leaves us with is: Nothing is impossible.

***Marilyn August***
Santa Barbara News-Press
*March 11, 1997*

It is wonderful to have dreams and goals, yet things don't always turn out as we had wished. The best-laid plans, the best-formed goals, and the best-fashioned dreams are sometimes dashed by circumstances beyond our control. Perhaps there is a purpose for everything . . . even overcoming unfulfilled expectations. How does one deal with shattered dreams? What do you do when you cannot control what has happened? One thing we can control is our attitude. When tragedy, failure, and setbacks occur, we have the option of turning those liabilities into incomparable assets. Janine Sheperd's story shows how she took a devastating tragedy and turned it into a triumph.

# Learning to Fly

Australia

&#8658; &#8676;

*I am only one; but still I am one. I cannot do everything, but still I can do something. I will not refuse to do something I can do.*

### *Helen Keller*

Janine Sheperd has long pursued uncommon dreams. While her hometown of Sydney is a place of surf and sun, Janine found her passion on snow. A champion athlete, she was determined to win her country's first medal in the unlikely sport of cross-country skiing. She said that she "wanted to show the world that an Aussie could ski, could be the best at winter sports." But that unusual dream ended during a training bike ride in 1986. Janine's bicycle was hit by a truck. The accident broke her back and neck in four places and nearly killed her. Hospitalized for five months, the elite athlete could no longer feel her legs and feet. They told her if they did not operate she could be in a wheelchair the rest of her life. If they did operate there was a small chance she might walk again with calipers and a walking frame. Janine survived several surgeries and forced her body to move again. A new dream fueled her slow recovery, an ambition that even she admits seemed ridiculous. "It was a crazy thing. I've never wanted to fly in my life, but I just looked up and I thought, that's it, I can't walk, so I might as well fly."

Incredibly, just six weeks after her release from the hospital and still wearing a body cast, Janine took her first flying lesson. She says that she "got some funny looks, this skinny thing, limping around the place, covered in a big slab of plaster. People looked at me and thought, who is she kidding?" Remarkably, she controls the plane's pedals without being able to feel her feet. She relies on upper leg strength and plenty of concentration. Even with her physical limitations, Janine wanted more than a private pilot's license; she earned a commercial license, then became a flight instructor. Still, the sky was no limit; she took on aerobatic flying, and she is so good that she teaches that as well. Flying, she says, is freedom: "I love the feeling of being able to do whatever I want to do. Just dancing in the clouds."

Doctors said she would probably never walk or have children, but, determined to prove them wrong, Janine accomplished both. Today she and her husband Tim have two daughters and a son. The woman who set out to represent her country at the Olympics has instead inspired Australia with the perseverance and courage that defines a champion.

*Janine Sheperd*
Today

The cycle of life is one of the universal experiences of being human. We pass the light on to those who follow in our footsteps. It isn't always easy to understand the imprints of life on the body since life shows us the passage of time like a roadmap on our skin. We cannot prevent the passage of time, but we have the ability to see ourselves in a different light. J. Nozipo Maraire shares with us a moment between mother and daughter.

# A Letter for My Daughter

Zimbabwe

⇒ ⇐

*Love has nothing to do with what you are expecting to get, it's what you are expected to give—which is everything.*

**Anonymous**

I remember on the eve of my wedding, as I was nervously trying on my dress for the twentieth time, your father's mother slipped into my bedroom and locked the door. In the olden days, a woman returned to her parents' home, where the wedding took place. And so I had dutifully arrived in Chakowa three days earlier to begin preparations for the feasting and dancing that would precede and follow the traditional ceremony.

I was already uneasy, but the appearance of my mother-in-law-to-be at that hour fixed me in a state of catatonic terror. She stood at the door, stooped over her cane, her gray hair bundled in a majestic headdress, robed in a bright floral flannel nightgown, and simply stared at me. She did not smile or move for a full two minutes. Then she hobbled to my side and, taking my hand, guided me to the bed.

"Come, my child. Sit down. I have something to show you." My head reeled. I had had so little private contact with her up to this point. She was notorious for being a stubborn, cantankerous old woman whose displeasure could be amply displayed but not readily allayed. On that night, especially, I wanted nothing to go amiss. I was petrified that, like so many mothers-in-law, she was going to offer me herbs or charms for fidelity, desire, or fertility. What would I do? How could I gently but firmly decline the offer without appearing like an uppity city girl? I looked about, desperately wondering where Linda was; she was, after all, supposed to be helping fit the dress, but as usual my little sister was nowhere to be found when I needed her. To my horror and surprise, the old lady began to unbutton her gown. Slowly and painfully, the gnarled, arthritic hands began to reveal what was better left hidden. Before I looked away in embarrassment, I caught a glimpse of her breasts, pendulous and glistening but shriveled like giant black prunes, hanging from her bony frame.

"Now, you have the beauty of youth, so you can shudder at my wrinkled breasts," she said, chuckling to herself. Her grin was accentuated by a few remaining teeth hanging from thick pink-and-brown-speckled gums. I was now at an utter loss as to how to respond to her. She continued, "But just you wait and see, as the seasons pass, your waist shall grow thicker, your hips shall be round and full like the moon, and your breasts will hang low like fruit that has passed its ripeness on the tree." Now that her breasts were fully exposed, I was trying to look away yet not offend. She clasped my right hand in hers. Then she laid it on her wrinkled cheeks and made me caress each crevice. I could feel the roundness of her face, the soft bristles of her eyebrows, and the undulations of her forehead as she guided my hand gently over her entire profile. As she did so, she spoke softly.

"That was from the tears I shed at his birth. *Here hamma we!* It was painful. It hurt like the lightning that splits the trees. It made me want to sing and cry all at the same time. Right there—that line was when he began to talk. Oh, how I laughed and laughed! That furrow there—yes, there—feel how deep that is. That was when he left the farm and joined the struggle. Dear God, how I worried. Oh, and that little crease, that is from grinning at the sweet memory of his success. And that one—ooh, it hurts still there; don't press so deep—that was when they threw him into the jail, and they beat him because he tried to defend the boys that were fighting for our freedom." She sighed so deeply, I thought she was going to cry. But she only shook her head sadly and slipped my hand down her leathery skin to enfold her breast.

"This is where the strength of your man comes from. This is where he would crawl, grabbing at my blouse, howling for milk. I breast-fed six children, my dear! All greedy and strong. *He-He.*" She rubbed them gently. I was grateful when she let my hands go and began to cover herself.

"You look at us old women, covered from head to toe in our tight headdresses and our long skirts, and you think we are like the nuns, afraid to show their bodies because it is a sin. But that is not so. It is because we understand nature's ways. We have lived long and deep in the bush with her. And she is a woman like us. My beauty is here now," she said, pointing to her wrinkles and her breasts. "There are birthmarks and then there are these *He-He*. These are the marks of life. My face, just as it is, the map of my toils and joys, is as precious to me as your little waist and your rounded breast are to you. This is testimony to the love I have given my family. There is not a mark here that is my own. It belongs to Babava, Tapiwa, Chipo, Farai, Tawona, and Ziyanai. It is a body of love. You will see it as an old, dry, lifeless thing, but one day you will understand that each beauty has its season. The flaky, rough coconut protects the flesh and the sweet juices within. The body of youth knows its day and must live it to its fullest. The body of the harvest, too, has its time. That is mine. It is a body that has reaped and sown and gathered unto itself. Someday, too, will come the body of the earth, the final eternal one, which has no form or end, to which we must all return. I came to see you tonight, daughter, to tell you these words that my mother-in-law told me on my wedding night, ages ago, so that the wisdom of our ancestors may swell and ripen with each new bud that flowers. So our roots grow deeper and out words never die." At the mention of those deceased, she crossed herself and sat silent for a moment. As she began to redress, she whispered on in a more cheerful voice.

She told me as I sat frightened like a mouse, just like you, "A woman's body follows the moon. It is not still and hard like a man's. Her happiness and sadness take many forms; each day the brightness of her light and the mysterious depths of her shadows may change. A woman is close to the earth yet near to the heavens. She grows like the harvest; she becomes ripe like fruit. When, after many children, my son looks at you and asks where is the beauty of your youth, and the body of the harvest, that is the body of your later years. Look at nature, how she dresses herself for every season. In the summer, she adorns herself as fields of rose and pink blooms, with fruits of peach, mango, and lemon, and as the season cools, she, too, dresses in darker hues of brown, maroon, and gold, and in rains she is all gray mist and stormy blues. A woman must always be proud and look after herself. Those principles we follow forever, even us old ones." At that, she began to cackle loudly. She tapped her cane on the floor and rose with a heave.

"Good night, my dear girl. You will make my son happy, I know, and you will be a daughter we can be proud of." And with that, she unlocked my door, took my candle, and left me in complete darkness. I was stunned. I was at once charmed by the beauty of her words and frightened by their meaning. There was something of an honor in the intimacy of transcending the barriers erected by pride, decorum, and custom. She had shown off her body as a magnificent monument of the human spirit over hardship. How I wished then that my body, too, if it had to droop and shrivel, for surely everyone's did, would furl and desiccate with grace to sculpt the victory of my spirit; that I too, when heavy and bent with age, could caress my wrinkled lids and hold my sagging flesh as a majestic robe of a life well lived.

*J. Nozipo Maraire*
Zenzele

The first requirement for being human is that you will receive a body. You must have a body in order to navigate around the board game of life. Some people spend their entire lives wishing their bodies were different than they are. Other people ignore their body, pretending it isn't there or turning a deaf ear to its needs and requests. Other people mistreat or abuse their bodies. Yet there are others who honor and respect the body they received. Regardless of which category you may fall into, one of the greatest gifts you can give is the sharing of your own body with another. Bernard Lernout tells one of his family stories that illustrates . . .

# The Ultimate Gift

Belgium

⇒ ⇐

*Do all the good you can, by all the means you can, in all the ways you can, in all the places you can, at all the times you can, to all the people you can, as long as ever you can.*

**John Wesley**

In the spring of 1992, we faced our worst fears. Lisa, our eldest daughter had just turned eighteen. She was officially a woman, being launched into the spring of her life when we were told that her leukemia had relapsed. This was not the ideal birthday present. I believed we had conquered this disease. Now it reared its cruel and ominous head in the middle of our celebration of life. I kept asking "Why now? Why Lisa? Why our family?"

The doctors told us that a bone marrow transplant was required. This is a very painful and difficult ordeal for both patient and donor. The questions chased each other around my brain. Where would we find a donor? Would Lisa survive the trauma and pain? How costly would the procedure be? Could we afford it? Would there be enough money left for the other five children who also needed our resources? These questions swirled from my brain to my wife's and back again. Questions without immediate answers are the ones that torment and cause sleepless nights. I wondered what could happen to turn this crisis into a blessing.

One evening as I sat reading in my study, our youngest daughter, Eva, peeked her head in the door.

"Dad, may I have a moment with you?"

"Of course, Eva, what's on your mind?"

"I was wondering, I mean, I'm young and well, maybe my marrow is a match for Lisa."

I couldn't believe my ears, "You are volunteering to go through this painful process to save your sister's life?"

"I don't know if I'm a match, but I'd do anything to help Lisa."

I stared at Eva for the longest time. "Let's talk to the doctor tomorrow. We'll have you tested and see if it is possible. This is very kind and courageous of you to offer. Thank you." As I sat there, I felt blessed to have children who would think to offer their own pain and suffering to save their sibling's life.

The next day, Eva was tested and found to be the perfect match with Lisa's bone marrow. It was our second gift. Next, we had to prepare for the grueling surgery. Preparations were extensive, and day by day, physical, mental, and emotional adjustments filled our life with the focus of a possible miracle. The day before the procedure, we stood outside the radiation room, talking to Lisa on a microphone, while she underwent total body radiation. I felt tightness in my throat, a knot in my abdomen, burning in my eyes, and a surreal feeling surrounding my head, as if I couldn't believe this was really happening to our family. Finally the day was upon us. There it was: the special treatment room where we could only enter one at a time. Dressed in surgical attire, disinfected and scrubbed, I entered the room. I sat and watched the stream of life-giving cells extracted from Eva's hipbone trickle down a tiny plastic tube in the intravenous valve attached to Lisa's shoulder. The doctor's voice broke the deadening silence, "It will now take one hundred days, one hundred critical days before we will know if the bone marrow transplant was successful." Almost four months before we could relax, breathe easy, and hopefully give thanks. This was just another step in a long, slow process that would test our faith, hope, and love.

It was summer when the phone rang. It was the doctor with news. As I held my breath and braced myself, the words came through the phone, "It has been one hundred days. The BMT was a success. Your prayers were answered." I dropped the phone as the whole family rushed in to find out what had happened. I couldn't speak. My wife grabbed the phone and the doctor repeated the message. She told all the children that Lisa was going to live. Hugs, tears, kisses, and cheers rang out from our home.

As we sat in the garden, we popped a bottle of champagne and as the cork flew high into the sky, we all saw the silhouette of a huge bird; an eagle flew over our heads. This is a rare sight in Belgium. The eagle was a sign to me of freedom from the fear of the worst experience one can have in life. We were spared. We were blessed, and Eva gave her sister the greatest gift there is.

*Bernard Lernout*

Some people receive a body that appears to be a blessing while others receive what appears to be a challenge. Some are blessed with extraordinary beauty, while others appear to be plain, in constant pain, or have serious physical issues. Regardless of the beauty, functionality, or difficulties you experience with your own body, the lessons are there to teach us something very specific. Each body is not only a gift to be used for our own personal development, it can also be used to help others on their path. This story is shared with us by Keith Fleshman and illuminates how one person's journey impacted an entire community.

## Mahaba

Ethiopia

➣ ⌖

*Whatever you are, be a good one.*

**Abraham Lincoln**

"Mahaba, eight years old, female, orphaned, from Gondar, for burn rehabilitation."

These were the only words written on her medical history and biography when she was brought to us at the leprosy hospital. The brevity was because of the frustration they must have felt. The medical staff at Gondar had saved her life, but what is life to a child with no family?

Mahaba walked half-upright, apelike, hips and knees bent due to scars on her backside. Having no elastic armpit skin, her arms were tightly attached to both her sides. Scars on her neck and face pulled her chin and part of her lower lip to her chest, forcing her mouth open in a perpetual snarl. To chew her food she ducked her head, bobbing it up and down to move the mobile head against the immobile lower jaw. Her ears were missing. Contracted eyelid scars kept her staring, eyes open, day and night. When awake, she rolled her eyes up, moving the iris out of sight to moisten her delicate corneas. At night the nurses moistened her sleeping, unprotected eyes with artificial tears, hour after hour.

Though her face said nothing, her body spoke for her. She retained the ability and the need to snuggle. She was only eight. When you are eight, hurt, and homeless, the most healing of all medicines is a hug. The nurses and the doctors, when involved with paperwork, often felt a shadow creep in the room. A tiny, warm, little body slid in under the available arm, huddled into the hollow of their shoulder, snuggled, sighed, and sniffed when squeezed a bit, and then slipped off through the ward to help some less mobile patient.

Mahaba came to us because the leprosarium was equipped for plastic surgery, brace-making, and for long-term care. The hospital became Mahaba's home. The entire staff became her family.

Gradually and repeatedly, swatches of soft, unburned skin was robbed off a half-layer of epidermis to resurface areas of fat and muscle to free up her neck and joints. We stitched ellipses of full-thickness skin as grafts into lips, upper eyelids, and lower eyelids, allowing her to lift her chin, shut her mouth, and shut her eyes while sleeping.

As she grew, she outgrew the surgical corrections, requiring repetition of the repairs. Mahaba filled the times of waiting with work, learning to sew, to embroider, and to do patient care. We stopped seeing the gargoyle because the sweetness of her person outshone her scars.

Across town, in a large, rented house, Reverend Jack Smith (always known simply as Mr. Jack) had collected a community of street boys. These lads, aged from five to eighteen years old, had been orphaned or abandoned, mostly due to the famine in the north, and had drifted to the streets of Addis. There they did odd jobs, washed cars, sorted garbage, carried burdens, begged, stole, or intimidated passersby. They did whatever they had to do to survive.

Every day they siphoned a little gasoline from one parked car or another. Even though Addis Ababa has an altitude of 7,500 feet, and is located quite near the equator, the streets were very cold at night. When your bed is a park bench, a bus kiosk, or a sheltered corner in an alley, it is easier to sleep if you are anesthetized by sniffing gasoline fumes.

One of these lads, when interviewed by Mr. Jack, described his fate like this: "God made everything and put everything into its own place. When he created men, he created each with his own work. The work of some men is to be soldiers, for some, it is to be king. The work of some is to grow food from the soil, for others, to sell it, and for many to eat the food that is grown. None of this work is my work; neither to be a king nor to eat food, my work, my destiny is only to suffer."

Because he was neither indifferent nor strong enough to ignore this suffering, Mr. Jack decided to do something about it. Through explaining, persuading, cajoling, and ultimately begging he put together a local organization of compassionate men who funded a rescue mission. They named it "Hope for Boys." The center enabled boys to attend school, live in a community, learn a trade, and become productive citizens. After their experience at Hope for Boys, they reentered society as providers rather than parasites.

Mahaba's surgery rate gradually decreased. Eventually, she needed only a couple of touch-up surgeries each year. It became unreasonable for her to have a permanent home in the hospital. But what alternative did she have?

Arranging a marriage with someone who would care for and cherish her seemed impossible. Finding a place as a household slave to be hidden in the back rooms was possible. But we could never submit her to a life of working in rags and feeding on scraps.

Mahaba had learned to suffer. In being comforted, she had leaned to comfort. She went to live as a servant girl at the center. At Hope for Boys, there was a constantly changing stream of little ones who needed, as she had needed, a hug, a cuddle, or an arm around them. There, she who would probably never be a mother, became a mother to many young boys. There, in that home, she became beautiful. For no boy has an ugly mother.

*Keith Fleshman, M.D.*

The whispers of the soul are intuitive messages that provide clear direction for our lives. Messages come to us in a variety of ways. Sometimes they are obvious, while other times they are camouflaged. The people closest to us don't always approve of the actions that make our hearts sing. Yet ultimately, each one of us must make our own choices about our bodies. It is up to us to make the choice that gives us peace and serenity. Shubhra Agrawal shares her story of someone listening to her messages regardless of what others think.

# Mr. Vijay Goel

India

⇒ ⇐

*The good deed you do today for brother or
sister in need will come back to you someday,
for humanity's circle indeed.*

### *Robert Alan*

Mr. Vijay Goel always surprised me with his unexpected yet delightfully affectionate outbursts. I relished the time I spent with him, playing games and horsing around. I, of course, loved the attention he gave me.

He was so childlike in his enthusiasm, as we shared many experiences, and spent untold hours discussing the meaning of life. He believed life was an experiment that encouraged learning at every juncture. He loved the most simple and ordinary, yet at times did what appeared to be the most extraordinary.

Years passed and without my noticing, I became a teenager. One summer, Mr. Goel invited me to join him on a journey to a special camp. I was slightly hesitant at first because none of my brothers or sisters (five of them), were able to come. His enthusiasm convinced me that it would be the right thing to do. When I decided to join him, I had no idea what lay ahead of me.

He had joined a group of activists who were trying to reshape a community in a backward village called Bishumpur in the state of Bihar (India). The locals living there were the Adivasis tribe. He and his team were various professionals from different fields of education, medicine, agriculture, and psychology.

I thought I was just accompanying Mr. Goel on one of our usual fun-filled adventures. Little did I know that this particular excursion was going to be an emotional encounter leaving a lifelong impression on me. The journey was long and tiring.

Mr. Goel proved to me that progress is made by intermingling one's values and intentions. These people carried on with their daunting work of breaking through communication barriers and endeavoring to improve the living conditions of the Adivasis, the local tribe; they encountered every reaction with both passion and devotion.

Mr. Goel felt confident of his ability to overcome obstacles. I had no idea of the dream that he had in his mind. I watched him open the treasure chest of his innermost thoughts and feelings.

Facing problems of all sorts, making little or no headway in finding solutions, he pioneered a project that is making a difference.

One day he came across an advertisement in the paper. It was an appeal to save someone's life with a kidney donation. He decided to donate his kidney to the person who placed the ad in the paper. He wanted no remuneration, or acknowledgment for his generous act, nor did he discuss his decision with anyone because he wanted to avoid possible criticism.

He completed all the medical tests. Time passed quite rapidly and before he knew it, it was time for the surgery. He booked his plane ticket and reserved his hotel. Before leaving for the hospital in Hyderabad, some 2,000 km from Delhi, he casually mentioned to me that he was going to donate his kidney to a stranger. He made me promise that I would keep the information confidential.

I received a note written a night before the operation. It said, "It's important not to feel weak before a test." Sharing what was heartfelt was the next block in building our relationship. For the next three days, Mr. Goel was missing.

All of his family members questioned me. Mr. Goel was very clear he wanted to make his own decision. I was torn between my loyalty to him and revealing the truth. Up to this moment, this had been the most intense experience of my life.

Finally the day arrived when he returned home, barely recovered from the surgery. All his family members waited to receive him and bombard him with questions. I watched him enter the hall and set his briefcase down on the floor. His gentle voice leaked through cherished greetings. My heart pounded. I looked up into his eyes, his head lowered, and I saw in his eyes the joy in his spirit, and then in a flash his white teeth revealed a huge smile. I knew he had followed his heart. He knew from the look in my eyes that I had honored his secret. I secretly celebrated with him.

The art of giving selflessly is a precious lesson. I learned it from watching someone give for no reason to a total stranger. Mr. Vijay Goel was my role model, but even more important, he is my father.

*Shubhra Agrawal*

L ife is a gift, yet all people don't always act as if they believe this truth. Pain and suffering have a value, yet it is not often clear what purpose they serve. The question of who gets to live and who gets to die is not up to us. Although it is wrong to intentionally take a life, we can knowingly preserve one. It is within our authority to use our power to make a difference. Pamela Daugavietis shares her miracle story that truly made a difference in a stranger's life.

# Facundo's Miracle

Argentina

➣ ➣

*It is when you give of yourself that you truly give.*

**Kahlil Gibran**

"I'm alive," said Denise Tamminga, thirty-seven, as she awoke following surgery on June 4, 1996. By the time her anesthesia wore off, her bone marrow was on its way from Ann Arbor, Michigan, to Israel. All she knew of the recipient was that he was a five-year-old boy suffering from Wiskott-Aldrich Syndrome, a rare genetic disorder, and that her gift might possibly save his life.

Denise yearned for a way to transform the painful loss of her father from leukemia, in 1991, into the gift of life for someone else.

In the spring of 1994, when her local blood bank was seeking donations for a little girl dying of leukemia, Denise got her first chance. Unfortunately, Denise's blood was not a match for the little girl, and the little girl passed away.

On August 21, 1994, the day before the third anniversary of her father's death, Denise got a second chance to turn her grief into joy. She received a call from the blood bank near her Holland, Michigan, home. The caller told Denise her marrow type matched that of a child who desperately needed a transplant.

"The lady told me I was one of approximately five hundred people in the world whose marrow was a possible match. She asked if I would be interested in donating. I couldn't believe she was calling the day before the third anniversary of my dad's death and that the little boy was three years old. I took it as a sign that I should say 'yes.'

Over the next year or so, Denise gave many more blood samples. The donor bank said they would call her when the time was right.

Finally, in the spring of 1996, the call came. Denise's bone marrow was a perfect match. The little boy, now five years old, had been awaiting a transplant since birth. Denise signed a letter of agreement binding her to fulfill her promise to donate, since chemotherapy and radiation in preparation for surgery would leave the little boy defenseless against infection.

Bone marrow donors and recipients cannot contact each other until both parties agree to reveal their names, at least one year after the procedure.

Three months following Denise's surgery, the blood bank called, saying the little boy, whose name was still confidential, was recovering and doing well. "He's alive! The little boy is alive," Denise tearfully and gratefully shouted to her family as she hung up the phone.

"We had been praying for him every day, asking God to keep him alive and to make him well," said Denise. "Our prayers were answered."

And then, in July 1997, the letter Denise had hoped for arrived from Santiago Del Estero, Argentina, written by a translator.

*Dear Denise: My name is Facundo and I'm six years old. A year ago, I got a bone marrow transplant in Israel after waiting for it for five years. My parents and I are eternally grateful to you for your action. We wish to meet you and hug you and kiss you.*

*I'm in the first grade. I'm going to learn English so I can keep in touch with you. I like playing ball, riding my bike, and fishing. I have a lot of energy after the transplant. In the future, I'll tell you more about myself and will be waiting for your answer. We all send you a big kiss. Facundo Lucca and parents.*

Overjoyed to hear from Facundo, Denise answered his letter right away. In October, a response from Facundo's mother arrived, also written by a translator.

In her heartfelt four-page letter, Teresita Lucca wrote, "We know our miracle has a name—Denise." She called Denise "the tool that God gave us to save the life of our only son." She told of her unceasing prayers, asking God to save Facundo's life. Facundo's older brother, Ignacio, had died of the same genetic disorder that threatened Facundo's life, until Denise's bone marrow saved him.

Still, the Tammingas yearned to know more about Facundo, his hometown, and way of life. They wanted to speak with the Lucca family, to perhaps arrange a visit. But as the Tammingas do not speak Spanish, they couldn't even make a phone call to the family in Santiago Del Estero.

When Dr. Luis Tomatis, a Grand Rapids heart surgeon, heard of Denise's plight, he was delighted to help. A native of Argentina, Dr. Tomatis was surprised to learn that Facundo and his family live in the city where Dr. Tomatis's mother was born, and where three of his nieces live today.

Dr. Tomatis immediately telephoned the family and spoke with Enrique, Facundo's father. To their mutual amazement, they realized they had met years earlier at a conference in Argentina. The Luccas were seeking medical help to save their oldest son, Ignacio. Dr. Tomatis, who presented the lecture they attended, gave them information that eventually led them to Israel for Facundo's bone marrow transplant. At the time, Israel was one of the few countries in the world offering the type of transplant Facundo needed.

Within a year, Facundo and his parents were invited to appear on Argentina's popular TV program, *Surprise and a Half,* and totally surprised Denise and her family when Facundo suddenly appeared at the Tamminga home last summer.

When the show aired in Argentina two months later, Denise and two of her children were guests of the show's producer in Buenos Aires, as a surprise to Facundo and his parents. A record audience of six million viewers watched the video of Denise and Facundo's tearful meeting in Michigan. The momentum created by the show led to an increase in bone marrow donations now available for transplant in Argentina.

"It such a small world," said Dr. Tomatis, still amazed by the global chain of events that may lead to the lives of many more children like Facundo being saved.

The Tammingas and the Luccas call them a chain of miracles.

*Pamela Daugavietis*

If everything in life were perfect, there would be little to learn. It is through adversity and challenge that we discover who we are. Some of us do very little with what we have while others do an enormous amount with hardly anything at all. Perhaps it is the person who makes miracles happen and doesn't think twice that truly inspires us to not only be grateful for what we have, but who inspires us to transcend our limitations as well. In her story, Lois Logan Horn lets us take a close look at someone who lets nothing stop her.

# Nobuko

Japan

➤ ◄

*Existence in itself, taken at its least miraculous, is a miracle.*

### Rebecca West

I had just returned from a year in Japan. I had learned some Japanese and had the rich and wonderful experience of learning about another culture, set of customs, and people. When my boss came into my office one morning and told me we would have a visitor from Japan the next day, I was delighted to extend the same hospitality that I had received.

The woman coming to visit was named Nobuko, and she and I were both social workers. I was looking forward to learning from her what she saw as our cultural differences and similarities.

Nobuko's job was placing adoptive and foster children in homes. She had won a prize for distinguished service as a caseworker in Japan. I found that Nobuko was passionate about everything she encountered. She took her job seriously and felt great pride when the children she placed were a perfect match with the families she selected. Nobuko had many interests; however, most tasks were very difficult for her. She had learned how to cook, sew, embroider, and do calligraphy.

The remarkable thing about Nobuko was that she had accomplished so much despite the fact that she had no hands. Nobuko had lost her forearms in an accident with a power saw when she was five years old. When she was reaching for firewood to take to her family she tripped and fell into the saw. She was determined, however, to live a "normal" life.

Nobuko showed me that we can transcend limitations and fulfill all our dreams.

*Lois Logan Horn*

Each life has a purpose and a timeline. We cannot know the grand scheme of things from merely our own point of view. There are no accidents and all things happen for a reason even when they seem to make no sense at all. In this story one family's tragedy becomes another family's blessing. Transcending loss means aligning with a higher purpose. Embracing what life has to give means surrendering to what is and learning the larger lesson.

## And the Beat Goes On

Israel

⇒ ⇐

*Peace will require greater understanding and respect for differences within and across national boundaries. We humans do not have the luxury any longer of indulging our prejudices and ethnocentrism. They are anachronisms of our ancient past. The worldwide historical record is full of hateful and destructive behavior based on religious, racial, political, ideological, and other distinctions—holy wars of one sort or another. Will such behavior in the next century be expressed with weapons of mass destruction? If we cannot learn to accommodate each other respectfully in the twenty-first century, we could destroy each other at such a rate that humanity will have little to cherish.*

**Carnegie Commission on the Prevention of Deadly Conflict**
**Robert S. McNamara,** Argument without End

In a tiny village in Saudi Arabia, doctors advised the Jaroushi family that their daughter, who had an enlarged heart, would die within a few weeks. Their only hope was if, by some remote chance, a heart with matching blood type could be found in time.

Reem Al Jaroushi, a tiny, three-year-old Arab girl was waiting for the heart that could save her life. Her parents were only too aware that it would take nothing short of a miracle for their daughter to live. They prayed daily for the miracle that could save Reem's life. It would mean finding the heart that could match her blood type and integrate with her tissue, all before the appointed date. As the computers searched for a match, they found nothing. It seemed more and more hopeless with each passing day.

Yom Kippur is the "day of atonement." It's the Jewish holiday when Jews ask God to forgive all the wrongdoings from the past year. It's also the day their fate is "sealed" for the coming year. The Kavehs are a Jewish family, who hold the holidays as a sacred time. An event occurred that day that would change their lives forever.

On the day before Yom Kippur, Yuval Kaveh, a vibrant eight-year-old boy, was walking in front of his parent's home in Tel Aviv. While crossing the street, Yuval was hit by a passing car. Yuval's parents frantically rushed him to the nearest hospital where he died just hours later.

At the hospital the doctors determined that Yuval's lifeless body held a healthy heart. After they examined the blood type, the doctors entered the information in the computer. In Saudi Arabia, the technicians who were watching hourly to see if a matching heart had been found saw the incredible information on their screen. The doctors and technicians discovered that this heart was the match they had been searching for. This heart that had its short life taken from it could now give life to another.

For a mother who had just lost a son, the importance was unquestionable. With selfless love, Yuval's parents donated his organs to the hospital. They gave, along with the physical heart of their son, their own loving hearts. The Kaveh family had lost the sweet gift of their child; however, they had given the matchless blessing of life to another child and her family.

Little Reem's family traveled to the home of Yuval's parents to thank them. When they entered the home of the family they could never sufficiently thank for the gift of life, they found them deeply grieving over the loss of their son. Seated in the den, they were watching a videotape of Yuval dancing at a family wedding. He was clowning around, smiling, laughing, and dancing with everyone. Reem's mother promised to bring her to visit her extended family often. Two families united with one heart. Yuval's mother said, "He had the heart of an angel, and now an angel has his heart."

Yuval's Jewish heart now pumps Reem's Arab blood. The talented doctor who performed the miracle surgery noted, "Inside all hearts look the same. It doesn't matter where it was taken from or to whom it was given; regardless of nationality, race, religion, or gender at our essence, we are all human beings."

***Tom Aspel***
Today

# RULE 2 TWO

## YOU WILL BE PRESENTED WITH LESSONS

*You are enrolled in a full-time informal school called "life."*
*Each day in this school you will have the opportunity to learn lessons.*
*You may like the lessons or hate them, but you have designed*
*them as part of your curriculum.*

We see through our own eyes, yet everything we see is a matter of perspective. It may seem as if the entire world can be seen in the macrocosm of your neighborhood, but knowing the big picture can shift reality. There are times when you must confront reality and see things as they truly are. The originator of the following piece of writing  has repeatedly been cited as either Dr. Philip Harter of Stanford University or, more often, simply "anonymous."

After extensive research, David Taub, a British journalist resident in the United States, discovered the identity of the person behind the concept of "The Global Village" and the original article, "Global Village of 1,000" (not the simplified version of one hundred in the e-mail).

The simplified version sent by e-mail, compared to the original version, pales by comparison. The original author was a remarkable woman, Donella (Dana) H. Meadows, who died on February 21, 2001. Donella Meadows was a professor at Dartmouth College, New Hampshire, and a highly accomplished author, lecturer, and environmental journalist. Her original "State of the Village Report" was published as follows.

# Global Village

Whole World

≫ ≪

*The earth is a beehive, we all enter by the same door.*

**African Proverb**

State of the Village Report

If the world were a village of 1,000 people:
584 would be Asians
123 would be Africans
95 would be East and West Europeans
84 Latin Americans
55 Soviets (still including for the moment Lithuanians, Latvians,
Estonians, etc.)
52 North Americans
6 Australians and New Zealanders

The people of the village would have considerable
difficulty communicating:
165 people would speak Mandarin
86 would speak English

83 Hindi/Urdu
64 Spanish
58 Russian
37 Arabic

That list accounts for the mother-tongues of only half the villagers.
The other half speak (in descending order of frequency) Bengali,
Portuguese, Indonesian, Japanese, German, French, and 200
other languages.

In the village there would be:
300 Christians (183 Catholics, 84 Protestants, 33 Orthodox)
175 Moslems
128 Hindus
55 Buddhists
47 Animists
210 all other religions (including atheists)

One-third (330) of the people in the village would be children.
Half the children would be immunized against the preventable
infectious diseases such as measles and polio.
Sixty of the thousand villagers would be over the age of 65.

Just under half of the married women would have access to and be using modern contraceptives.

Each year 28 babies would be born.

Each year 10 people would die, three of them for lack of food, one from cancer. Two of the deaths would be to babies born within the year.

One person in the village would be infected with the HIV virus; that person would most likely not yet have developed a full-blown case of AIDS.

With the 28 births and 10 deaths, the population of the village in the next year would be 1,018.

In this thousand-person community, 200 people would receive three-fourths of the income; another 200 would receive only 2 percent of the income.

Only 70 people would own an automobile (some of them more than one automobile).

About one-third would not have access to clean, safe drinking water.

Of the 670 adults in the village, half would be illiterate.

The village would have 6 acres of land per person,
6,000 acres in all, of which:
700 acres is cropland
1,400 acres pasture
1,900 acres woodland
2,000 acres desert, tundra, pavement, and other wasteland

The woodland would be declining rapidly; the wasteland increasing; the other land categories would be roughly stable. The village would allocate 83 percent of its fertilizer to 40 percent of its cropland—that owned by the richest and best-fed 270 people. Excess fertilizer running off this land would cause pollution in lakes and wells. The remaining 60 percent of the land, with its 17 percent of the fertilizer, would produce 28 percent of the foodgrain and feed 73 percent of the people. The average grain yield on that land would be one-third the yields gotten by the richer villagers.

If the world were a village of 1,000 persons, there would be five soldiers, seven teachers, one doctor. Of the village's total annual expenditures of just over $3 million per year, $181,000 would go for weapons and warfare, $159,000 for education, $132,000 for health care.

The village would have buried beneath it enough explosive power in nuclear weapons to blow itself to smithereens many times over. These weapons would be under the control of just 100 of the people. The other 900 people would be watching them with deep anxiety, wondering whether the 100 can learn to get along together, and if they do, whether they might set off the weapons anyway through inattention or technical bungling, and if they ever decide to dismantle the weapons, where in the village they will dispose of the dangerous radioactive materials of which the weapons are made.

"State of the Village" copyright is held by Sustainability Institute, Vermont, and reprinted with permission by the copyright holder.

*Donella Meadows and David Taub*

Many people focus on differences, yet some of us focus on similarities. It is up to us how we view those who are different from us. When we transcend race, gender, creed, and nationality, what is left is our humanity. In this we are all truly alike. In Maya Angelou's poem, she eloquently perceives the Human Family as one species, on one planet, striving to overcome our differences.

# Human Family

United States

⇒ ⇐

*Difficulties are meant to rouse, not discourage.*

### *William Ellery Channing*

I note the obvious differences
In the human family.
Some of us are serious,
Some thrive on comedy.

Some declare their lives are lived
As true profundity,

And others claim they really live
The real reality.

The variety of our skin tones
Can confuse, bemuse, delight,
Brown and pink and beige and purple,
Tan and blue and white.

I've sailed upon the seven seas
And stopped in every land,
I've seen the wonders of the world,
Not yet one common man.

I know ten thousand women
Called Jane and Mary Jane,
But I've not seen any two
Who really were the same.

Mirror twins are different
Although their features jibe, and lovers think
Quite different thoughts
While lying side by side

We love and lose in China,
We weep on England's moors,

We laugh and moan in Guinea,
And thrive on Spanish shores.

We seek success in Finland,
Are born and die in Maine.
In minor ways we differ,
In major we're the same.

I note the obvious differences
Between each sort and type,
But we are more alike, my friends,
Than we are unalike.

We are more alike, my friends,
Then we are unalike.

*Maya Angelou*
I Shall Not Be Moved

We will often go out of our way to help a family member or a friend, but how many of us go out of our way to help a total stranger? When you put yourself in another's shoes and understand their plight you display a rare quality. Doing random acts of kindness is not only reserved for family and/or friends, it is an aspect of our caring for every person on Earth . . . since we are ultimately all connected. In the following story, Bob Steevensz shares about going out of his way to help a member of the larger human family . . .

## Going the Extra Mile

The Netherlands

⋙ ⋘

*A person's true wealth is the good he or she does in the world.*

**Mohammed**

I hadn't seen my friend Juan for quite some time; he was very busy with his life, but tonight, he was going to be home and I was looking forward to our visit. I have always loved spending time with him, since he has a great sense of humor and he makes me laugh more than anyone else. I arrived at Juan's house at 9:15 P.M., and was surprised to find no one there. I thought it was odd, although I wasn't totally shocked, since Juan can be disorganized and forgetful. I called his mobile and home phones and left messages. Then I got back in my car but I didn't feel like going home. The night was still young. I decided to visit another old friend I hadn't seen for a while. I called his house, but the line was busy, so I decided to go downtown and walk around. When I paid for my parking space at the machine, a man approached and asked me a question.

He had a ticket in his hand and he was confused about the parking protocol. He was disturbed about the yellow clamp attached to his car that imprisoned his car. All three people with him seemed to be upset as well. I explained that they had to call the number on the ticket for someone to come and remove the clamp. I also mentioned that they would have to pay seventy euros. I asked if they had a phone with them, but they had neither a phone nor euro coins with which to use the public phone.

The man explained that he was from Romania, that his wife, his parents, and he were just passing through Amsterdam on their way to Antwerp, and they were on a tight budget. I offered to make the call for them on my mobile phone. It felt like the right thing to do for people who were clearly inconvenienced by this incident.

I tried in vain to negotiate between the parking service and the family. I wanted to help them. However, since the family didn't have a credit card (which is quite common in Romania), the service wasn't willing to send a truck to remove the clamp. In addition, the parking clamp people mentioned they wouldn't accept cash. They said it was against their policy.

At this point, the options were becoming more and more limited. They could either go to a special office outside of the city, pay the ticket, and have the clamp removed, or they could let the car stay there overnight and pay the fee the next morning at a nearby office. That meant that they would have to find lodging for the night. The man told me that they had to go to Antwerp tonight and find an inexpensive hotel outside the city.

The money they had to pay to have the clamp removed was equal to a month's salary in their country. They would be forced to shorten their trip because of this incident. This was really a mild catastrophe for them. The wife and the parents who spoke no English were looking very distraught.

The man asked me if I could help him. He asked if I had a credit card, and would pay the ticket and receive Romanian money back from him. I had no problem with that, although it meant I had to call the service again and ask for a car to come and wait for that, regardless of how long it took. At that point I had already spent quite some time with these people and the thought came to me that maybe I had been sent to help them. So I called the number and explained our strategy and was told that a truck would come in about half an hour.

I started pointing out that we could use the time waiting to see what we could learn from this whole situation. I said, "You can look at it as a disaster and have it ruin your time in Amsterdam or you can turn it around and make it into a positive experience." We talked about the fact that sometimes things happen that seem to get in our way and they throw us completely out of balance. We talked about my job, what I do with people, how to coach people through things that happen. He was clearly interested and seemed to lighten up during our conversation. We talked about growing up and being educated by parents and how difficult it is at times to cope with things that happen. I enjoyed talking to him.

The parking service eventually arrived to remove the clamp. At that moment I had a clear "message" to pay the ticket and let them keep their Romanian money. I got a thrill from the idea. When my new friend offered me the money after I paid their bill, I graciously refused it. He was in shock and insisted I take his money. His wife stood in disbelief with a huge smile on her face. To me that moment was worth much more than seventy euros.

The man wanted to know my name, so I gave him my card and told him, "Please do not send money. Do send a postcard to tell me about your trip and let me know you arrived home safely." We shook hands and I walked away feeling I had done the right thing helping a stranger solve his problem in a foreign city. I knew that his memory of Amsterdam would not be the expensive clamp and the inconvenience, but rather the Dutchman who went the extra mile.

***Bob Steevensz***

Few experiences are all good or all bad. It is often your personal perspective that colors an experience and makes it into your reality. Each one of us has the option to look for the good news in each situation or to continually search for what is wrong. If we expose ourselves to different points of view we can broaden our perspective. Each person can open the door to new possibilities as David Irvine opens the door in this story.

# There Are No Bad Days

Canada

➤ ◄

*Each day provides its own gifts.*

**American Proverb**

I was aboard a plane flying home to Canada. I travel a lot and I get pretty disgusted with the conditions in air travel these days. After being served my meal, I was ready to start complaining to the person next to me about the food, the uncomfortable seats, the delays, and the general inconvenience.

Before I opened my mouth, the woman sitting next to me spoke. She had a thick accent and in broken English she talked about the wonderful service she received on the plane. She then proceeded to comment on the cheerful flight attendants, and then she said, "We were fortunate to be having such a fine meal. I am so happy to be flying to Vancouver to visit my grandchildren." Amazed, I asked "How can you be so positive and optimistic in a world that seems so marginal?"

"I am from Sarajevo," she said. "I have seen my friends and many of my family killed. I joined my family here in your wonderful country. You see, the food on the plane, the delays, they don't matter to me. Since coming here, every day is a good day for me. I have learned that there are really no bad days anymore, only bad thoughts."

Her comment put everything into perspective.

***David Irvine***

Things happen in life that are completely unexpected. People act in unpredictable ways that we cannot control. The challenge is not in expecting people to conform to your ideas of how they are supposed to behave, but rather in going to a deeper place and connecting with their essential self. Elizabeth Zamerul Ally shares how miraculous things happen when we reach out to each other in authentic ways.

## Transcending Fear

Brazil

⇒ ⇐

*They may forget what you said, but they will never forget how you made them feel.*

### Carl W. Buechner

It was already 8:30 P.M. when Rose stretched out to de-kink her tired body after those long hours at the office. She had finished her consulting work and was pleased with the results. After having locked the office, she was at the reception desk, the last one to leave, handing over the office key and waving good-bye to the doorman.

After rounding the corner of her building, she could just see her car in the distance. She realized that she might have been a little thoughtless, considering how deserted the area was at this time of night. When she got into her car she looked into the rearview mirror and noticed someone rapidly approaching her car. She just had time to close and lock the doors before the man reached her window and pointed a gun at her. It took Rose less than a second to make the decision that seemed obvious to her. Reluctantly, she opened the car door as the man nervously motioned her to move over into the passenger's seat. Rose moved over, feeling frightened but trying to move smoothly so as not to avoid frightening the man. He put his gun in his waistband, and sat in the driver's seat.

They soon left the garage, but he couldn't turn on the headlights, even after trying several times. He was becoming more and more irritated and nervous. The car model was new and unfamiliar to him, and he asked Rose for help. She said that her hand had to cross over the steering wheel in order to reach the switch. He agreed to her reaching for the switch and she patiently taught him how to turn on the headlights.

While he drove toward the outskirts of the city, there were infinitely long silent moments. Various scenarios began to flood her consciousness. Rose recalled the evening news and the innumerable situations that ended up in violence, rape, and finally death. She immediately felt terror in the pit of her stomach. She decided to put that thought completely out of her mind. She then remembered that her car was brand new, expensive, and had twenty-four huge installments left, with no insurance. Then she thought, "If he takes my car . . ." Panic seized her again for a brief second, then she decided to put that thought out of her head. She realized that she needed to replace those fearful thoughts with something more positive in order to maintain her composure. Then she remembered a passage from *Illusions* by Richard Bach: "There is no such thing as a problem without a gift for you in its hands. You seek problems because you need their gifts." She used this passage to calm herself down, breathing slowly, deeply, and deliberately. Then, she decided to break the silence.

"It is a nice car to drive, isn't it?" she said in a sweet, soft voice. Her tone did not match the situation, which confused her kidnapper. He reluctantly agreed and started to defend himself as someone who apologizes but does not feel repentant.

"Yeah, life is tough, ma'am  . . .  You have to get by!" Then, speaking up, he ordered, "Don't you dare shout, try to run away, or yell for the police. If you do, I'll shoot you!"

Using a low, calm tone, she assured him she would comply. She then asked him to calm down. It was quite obvious that he was more scared than she was. Paradoxically, it was he who needed to be comforted. On hearing her firm tone, he started to feel less tense. Rose wondered which gift she would be awarded for this experience. She had never faced anything like this, nor had she ever spoken to a criminal before. All of a sudden, she felt sincere interest in her assailant. She thought, who is this desperate man? What stories would he have to tell? Rose suddenly felt compassion for him. She looked at him for a while, avoiding staring at him because she thought this might increase his nervousness. She saw him as basically a good man, trying to survive. She also thought that he was sowing seeds of evil that he would harvest later. She also saw a man in conflict, restless, frightened, uncomfortable in his skin as either villain or victim. Suddenly, Rose began to ask him questions about his life. The man was amazed at her interest in him. How many victims would show any interest in their aggressor's life at a time like this? He started to tell her his story.

He told her he came from a much poorer state, where he had joined a gang of car thieves. He said the police had killed five of the eight and the remaining three had come to São Paulo. His two other friends had also died here so he was the only one left from the gang. When he said that, Rose noticed bitterness and grief in his voice, as if he could foresee his own death. He talked about the different types of criminals, bragging to her as if he wanted to impress her. He also shared that he loved his wife and children, for whom he had to provide. He confessed that he was a failure as a house painter. Once in a while he got a temporary job, but he hadn't been employed for two months and he had no rent money. He couldn't wait any longer for another job and had to return to his previous criminal life to get some money for his family. Rose listened to him attentively and calmly, without interrupting him. Sometimes she asked him questions to better understand his story. She seemed to have forgotten that he was a kidnapper.

When they reached her bank, they could easily see the twenty-four-hour ATM. A couple was withdrawing money. The man drove in the drive-through lane, stopped the car, and became very nervous again. He started threatening Rose, telling her she shouldn't dare let the couple know what was going on. He ordered her to get out of the car and withdraw the money while he closely watched her with his hidden gun aimed at her. She reassured him she wouldn't ask for help and while doing so, she opened the car door very carefully, got out, and went around the front of the car. At that moment she felt her heart thumping, as if she had been temporarily set free. She wished a police car would pass at that moment. She thought of signals she could send without being obvious and then abandoned the idea. She withdrew the money as she had been told and returned to the car.

The man started the engine, and noticing how calm she was, asked, "How can you be so calm and collected? I never met anybody like you!" Then, he started asking her questions about her life, whether she was married or not, where she was going. She told him she was divorced and she was on her way home.

He tried to convince her to give marriage a second chance, insisting that it would be awful to be alone at sixty. Whoever saw them talking in the car together would have thought they were two close friends driving and talking about their lives. He seemed to regret having kidnapped her, and so he attempted to comfort her,

"You know, ma'am, I ain't gonna steal your car. That wouldn't pay, anyway. The guys will pay very little for it. The police are more likely to come after me. People have a wrong picture of what criminals are like," he said, as if he resented such unfairness.

About forty minutes had gone by when he asked if she knew any road in the neighborhood where he could leave her, so that she could easily find her way home. She told him the directions and he drove her there. On reaching the road she had described, he stopped the car and asked her for the money she had withdrawn. As Rose handed him the money, she told him she deeply hoped he would change his lifestyle while he was still alive, then she wished him good luck. He then spoke to her in a rather tender way, as a father to his daughter.

"I also wish you good luck. Take care." Then, he looked at the fuel gauge and exclaimed, "You're almost out of gas. You can't get home on that. Here's some money for fuel." He quickly gave her part of the money he had just stolen from her. Then he got out of the car and, before running toward the woods, he looked at her with unforgettable pain and regret.

He was amazed and grateful for her attitude toward him, for her not having seen him as someone different from her. She overcame her fear and saw him as simply a human being. He may have been lost and desperate, but he was still a human being.

*Elizabeth Zamerul Ally*

Each person has his or her own individual lessons to learn. When you compare one person's lessons and tests with another's, it often doesn't seem fair that some people are given great gifts, while others seem to have major challenges. Each day 6,500 people—men, women, and children—die in Africa of AIDS. This is the story of Nkosi, whose life was filled with lessons and inspired all who met him.

## A Little Boy Who Inspired a Dream

South Africa

⟫ ⟪

*The purpose of life is not to be happy—but to matter, to be productive, to be useful, to have it make some difference that you have lived it all.*

**Leo Rosten**

Nkosi Johnson is twelve years old and dying of AIDS. Born HIV-infected on February 4, 1989, two years later he developed full-blown AIDS. Although doctors had given Nkosi nine months to live, he grew up and became a beacon of hope to millions of people living with HIV/AIDS not only in South Africa, but in many other parts of the world as well. Before he became sick, his mission was to stop others from becoming infected, and to look after those mothers and children who already were. With the help of his foster mother, Gail Johnson, Nkosi has spoken to the world about his life as a person living with HIV/AIDS. Because Nkosi was separated at a very young age from his HIV-infected mother, who was unable to look after him, he and his foster mother started a home for mothers and children living with HIV/AIDS.

Nkosi has taught people that those with HIV/AIDS are still valuable, loving, and generous human beings, and that there is no reason to avoid, ignore, or be afraid of them. Nkosi has endured more than most of us will in our lifetimes, and he's done it amongst all the prejudice and ignorance of a nation in the grip of fear. His tiny body doesn't do justice to the larger-than-life courage it houses, and while AIDS appears to have reduced him in size, this boy is still nothing less than a *giant.*

Now one of South Africa's longest-living children with AIDS, he's not only silenced the medical profession, but turned heads and opened hearts and eyes doing it. He has become an inspiration and an icon.

On December 29, 2000, Nkosi collapsed while bathing and was immediately rushed to the hospital. On January 6, 2001, after a week in the hospital, Nkosi was discharged after the doctors reached a decision that medically there was nothing else to be done for him. The diagnosis was permanent brain damage, and the doctors predicted that he was only going to live for six weeks, maximum. Yet Nkosi continued to live and celebrated his twelfth birthday. Unable to eat, talk, walk, or even turn himself over, he just lay in his bed waiting for his day to come.

Although Nkosi is aware that one day his time will come, he is proud of the fact that he will not have fought in vain. This courageous boy will leave a legacy behind, a legacy that will continue his struggle and forever keep his memory alive.

*Nkosi's Haven*

# RULE 3 THREE

# THERE ARE NO MISTAKES, ONLY LESSONS

*Growth is a process of experimentation, a series of trials, errors, and occasional victories. The failed experiments are as much a part of the process as the experiments that work.*

Things happen for a reason. At the time something happens, however, it is not always easy to see or understand the reason or purpose behind an event. It is only in hindsight that the reason something happened becomes clear to us. What may appear to be an accident can turn out to be quite serendipitous. Nupur Sen shares with us his "mistake" that turned out to be the perfect lesson.

# There Are No Accidents

Pakistan

⇒ ⇐

*When you make finding yourself—even if you're the last person on Earth to see the light—you'll never forget it.*

**Carl Sagan**

My grandfather was principal of a Christian missionary school in modern-day Pakistan. The house in which he lived had an outer door that was always unlocked. There was a flat on the ground floor and a flight of stairs that led directly to my grandfather's flat. Anyone who wanted to could enter his flat anytime.

My grandfather was educated; he spoke several languages and had volunteered to help the British doctors and the American missionaries translate English documents for the benefit of the Indian listeners. Over the years, many missionaries had spoken at the church.

One Thursday evening, the meeting at which the missionaries were speaking ran over the usual length of the service, in fact, it ended after 11:00 P.M. My grandfather arrived home quite late. He was annoyed to have the time agreements broken and to be delayed unnecessarily. However, when he reflected on the matter, he decided to simply let it go since it had never happened before.

The following week he returned from the service and was again delayed by what he perceived to be an overzealous preacher, who went on and on. When he came home, he was obviously irritated and decided to tell the missionaries that he was a busy man and needed to leave the church on time from then on. The missionaries apologized profusely and promised to keep to the agreed schedule.

The following Thursday the missionaries were again late ending the service and promised again to be punctual in the future. The following week the service was over at the regular time and he never had to speak to the missionaries about the problem again.

About three weeks later, as my grandfather bicycled down the road, he saw a young boy he recognized coming toward him on foot. They stopped and greeted each other as was the custom. Then my grandfather asked, "Why are you not in school?" The young boy looked down at the ground sheepishly and said, "I am not enrolled in any school. I had desperately wanted to attend your school, but when I met with the headmaster he turned me away. I was told that the principal had rejected my application."

My grandfather stared at the boy who continued to stare at the ground. After a moment of silence, the boy continued, "I had resolved to kill the man who had made this life-altering decision. On three consecutive Thursdays I went to your home and waited behind the stairs until 11:00. When you did not arrive, I left and went home. I was afraid that you had somehow figured out what I had planned."

These were the exact same days that grandfather had returned late from the church services. Grandfather stood there in shock. After an eternal moment of silence, Grandfather turned to the boy and took his face in his two hands. Weeping tears of remorse, he looked him in the eyes and asked, "Would you like to start school today?"

*Nupur Sen*

The are those moments, when "mistakes" happen and we question and wonder, "Why?" Razzan Zahra shares with us her "mistake" that ultimately turned into a "blessing." Whether we believe the incident is a mistake or not, it is presented as a test and if we pass it, we become rewarded. Razzan's story reminds us that asking for what you want can be very powerful.

## Values Passed On

Syria

➤ ◄

*The difference between greatness and mediocrity is often how an individual views a mistake.*

### Nelson Boswell

As a child, I often watched my grandma sit on her knees with her two palms facing the sky and her eyes toward the heavens. When she was done, she would take me by the hand and say, "Whenever you feel troubled or hurt, you simply ask God to take it away. When you feel lost, don't know what to do, get down on your knees and ask God to show you the way."

By the time I was in the first grade, the concept of trouble began to sink in. My parents sent me to what was then the best local school in

Damascus, Syria. I didn't feel comfortable or safe there. The teachers were stern and spent a big part of their day threatening to send bad kids to the basement they called "The Home of Rats." As a first grader I desperately needed a teacher's love and affection, but was reconciled to returning home without major punishments.

During recess and dismissal, there were many children who pushed and shoved each other. One day, I got caught in the midst of a crowd and as I was climbing the stairs, another child pushed me. Unable to maintain my balance, I stumbled and fell on my head. I was in so much pain that I lost consciousness and was rushed to a hospital. On my forehead, between my eyebrows, there was a round wound that revealed part of my skull. The doctors were afraid that it might have affected my brain.

Although the X ray revealed that there was no internal damage, I had never felt more insecure and frightened.

I struggled out of bed, sat down on my knees and prayed, "God, if you are listening, please help me. I don't feel okay. I am in pain. I want to go to a safe school with loving teachers and nice friends. I am tired of being afraid."

As soon as I said these words, I felt the severe pain in my head dissipate. A warm light swept through my body and calmed my weary heart, as if to say, help is on the way.

After a couple of weeks, my father received an internship that required us to move to Dallas, Texas, an internship he had been trying to get for over seven years. I went to Atherton Elementary School. It didn't have many students and the teachers were loving and supportive. There I spent some of the best years of my life. I realized that my prayer had been answered.

My grandma's advice became my truth. "Ask and you shall receive."

*Razzan Zahra*

Sometimes we make choices that look like mistakes. Things seem difficult or are fraught with challenges, and we start to doubt our clarity and decisiveness. When it looks as if we've made the wrong choice or decision we can waffle on our choices. Gunter David had such an experience. If we look at life as a series of lessons, we cannot make any mistakes, we can only learn lessons!

## Alien Soldier

United States

⇒ ⇐

*Only he who does nothing makes a mistake.*

**French Proverb**

"Left. Right. Left. Right.

"You had a good home when you left.

"You're right.

"Sound Off.

"One. Two. Three. Four."

I did have a good home when I left, I thought grumpily, marching in the sweltering heat of basic training. It was the Korean War and I was at Fort Dix Army Base in New Jersey. I had been drafted, trading a Manhattan apartment and a pretty dark-haired wife of twenty-two for a barracks full of guys. Why was I doing this? I often asked myself. After all, I wasn't even a United States citizen.

At eighteen I had come to America from Tel Aviv, Israel, where I grew up after my family fled Hitler's Germany. More than anything I wanted to be a newspaper reporter. It was a dream that went back to my childhood when my favorite movie was *The Front Page*. Sitting on the edge of my seat, I watched those reporters—flashing press passes, pounding the typewriter, racing deadlines all the way to a hot story with a byline. Someday that'll be me, I promised myself.

But it hadn't happened. I had graduated from journalism school, but couldn't get a job as a reporter. So I paid the bills by working as an inventory clerk. Then I was drafted. As a noncitizen, I could have easily escaped the army by refusing to pledge allegiance to the flag. But for me, accepting the draft was an act of faith in my new country. Becoming a reporter would have to wait.

The hardest thing was leaving my wife. The second hardest was trying to understand the corporal's flavor of English. He was from the south. My native tongue was German. My English was the New York brand.

"To the ri mach! To the le mach!" the corporal barked. "Sorry," I mumbled, slamming into the guy next to me. "Sorry," I said again, whacking into someone else.

"Halt!" bellowed the corporal. There was silence as he strode right to me, standing nose to nose. "Don't y'all speak English?"

I trembled. "N-noo." He stared at me in disbelief. "What y'all doin' in this man's army?" I hung my head. Unable to explain, I vowed to try harder.

What can I say about KP? I didn't know it stood for Kitchen Police. And when my name appeared on the duty roster under the heading Enlisted Men, I reasoned there had to be a mistake. After all, I hadn't enlisted. I was drafted. No such luck. I found myself in the mess hall peeling onions by the hour.

The last straw was garbage detail. Three mornings in a row I was singled out at reveille formation to work on the garbage truck. I started each day in clean khaki fatigues. My job was to stand in the back of the truck and dump garbage from cans hefted up to me by a regular army soldier. On the third morning, I grabbed a garbage can of leftover oatmeal. I turned it upside down, banging it against the side of the truck. Nothing happened.

"How do I get this stuff out?" I asked the soldier.

"Put your hand in it!" he commanded.

With bare hands I dug the slimy stuff, mixed with hair clippings from the Post barbershop, out of the can. It covered my boots, spreading in a pool around me. The truck lurched forward. I fell face down. I tried to get up, blindly slip-sliding in the mush. The hairy oatmeal covered me from head to toe. When I staggered into the noisy barracks that afternoon, silence filled the room. All eyes turned to me. Laughter erupted. There has to be something better than this, I thought.

There was. At reveille the next morning Sergeant Motley, the first sergeant, asked for volunteers who could type to step forward. Although I was a two-finger typist, I dashed ahead. Beating out several others, I announced breathlessly, "Private David reporting!"

I was marched to a stuffy, windowless room next to Motley's office. There I faced stacks and stacks of personnel records written in longhand. I was to type them up. My heart sank.

I sat down to my task. Day turned into night. I returned to the typewriter after chow and got to bed just before lights out. Yet I had hardly made a dent. I became a fixture in the room. I was excused from marches. I was excused from KP. My special status didn't sit well with my fellow soldiers. They ostracized me. Worse, they complained to the corporal.

One night I was on my top bunk in the barracks, feeling left out of the joking and laughter, my dream of being a writer still a million miles away. The corporal strolled in. There was silence. "Y'all listen to me. I'm tired of your grumbling. Private David here works hard," he drawled in a loud voice. "He puts in long, boring hours in that office. What's more, he's a college graduate."

Sheepish faces looked down. When the corporal left, those same faces turned up toward me, grinning awkwardly. An eighteen-year-old kid, who was so homesick he sometimes cried at night, broke the ice. He stepped forward, reticent.

"Private David," he said. "Can you write a letter for me? To my girl? I don't spell so good."

Others came forward and asked for help, too. They never again complained about my "special status."

By the time basic training ended, so had the fighting in Korea; an armistice was in place. I was transferred to Fort George G. Meade in Maryland where—miracle of miracles—I was assigned to work on the

*Post* newspaper. I received my first byline. I had a press pass. And, of course, plenty of deadlines. Just like in the movies. I knew I would do this forever.

One sunny morning, while I was still at Fort Meade, two buddies drove me to the Baltimore courthouse, where they witnessed my swearing-in as the newest U.S. citizen. Better even than my byline was the joy of finally being "officially" American. That big day was more than forty-five years ago. I still get shivers when I think of it.

After leaving the army, I went on to pursue a successful career in journalism. Those first days of basic training, lonely and depressed, I felt that I had been moving further and further from my dream. Now I know that the act of joining the army was simply paying a debt—in advance— to my new country. It was a small price to pay for a dream come true.

***Gunter David***

Sometimes the gifts we receive are camouflaged from us because of the packages they arrive in. The gift wrappings don't always match with our idea of what must be inside. In addition, our expectations sometimes block our ability to see something's true value. Martha L. Name gives us an example of gifts that arrived in unexpected packages.

# Stop and Listen

United States

⋙ ⋘

*If you judge people, you have no time to love them.*

**Mother Teresa**

Three years ago, when I took a job as manager at a low-income subsidized apartment complex in a Chicago suburb, I could never have imagined the impact that working with senior citizens would have on my life. As part of my job, I was to supervise and plan "social programming" activities to keep "my" senior residents occupied and entertained. Bingos, birthday parties, potlucks, health screenings, and craft classes were welcomed and appreciated. These special activities were great for them because they were fun! Yet I felt something was missing. I often pondered about how we were constantly developing ways to "keep the seniors busy," but now there were even greater needs to be responded to—the need for a sense of growth, relationship, and learning. There was the need to be heard and valued. Under one roof, so many people, with different backgrounds, experiences, and personalities! "How can I respond to these people on a personal level?" I asked myself. They gave me the answer . . .

It was a crazy Monday morning—phones ringing, tenants complaining: "My faucet leaks," "The closet door came off the track," "The sink is clogged." The deposits and accounting reports were due today, the boiler just broke down, maintenance and tenant problems were overwhelming. Mrs. Smith got drunk again last night and woke up the whole neighborhood, Mr. Lewis lost his job and can't pay the rent this month, on top of it all, contracts and paperwork to complete.

Mrs. Schultz, a plump, short, silver-haired seventy-three-year old, walks in and with a thick German accent says, "Here you go honey. A little something for your coffee," laying a hot, out-of-the-oven pile of cookies on my desk. With a smile on her face, she proceeds to sit down, making herself at home. "Let me tell you about my granddaughter. She got a scholarship you know. I am so proud of her!" And then with a solemn tone, she starts to tell me stories, about how her life used to be. "I always wanted to go to school, but wouldn't you know it, I fell in love with my Joe! He was the town butcher. I was very happy with my Joe. We had three children and always got the best cuts of meat! But I always wanted to learn."

Pretty soon I heard all about Joe, how they met, how they lived, how she felt when he died. She told me about her family and how she fled from Germany with her little brother many years ago. She complained about her health and how she rarely felt well anymore. She was once young and beautiful, and "as healthy as a horse!"

And here I am, with a million things to do. My morning is being consumed. A sense of frustration and impatience comes over me. I look at the mound of paperwork in front of me and then at this person sitting across from me, so engrossed in her own story, so happy to be heard. Here is a woman needing to share. Somewhere, deep inside me, the aggravation begins to lift and I relax, smile, and enjoy being this gem's audience of one. A sense of understanding and compassion fills me. What I have in front of me is Life itself—Life, needing to be acknowledged and responded to, needing to be heard; Life, an expression of the divine.

More and more, these kinds of encounters occurred. Gaining entrance to my office by bearing freshly baked goods and a smile, Mrs. Shultz opened the door for relationships to emerge with many wonderful people. I began to open myself up to these opportunities and to receive the true gifts these people were offering—the very fibers of their lives.

It was through the repetition of these encounters that I realized the need for a place and a space where "my seniors" could express their profound life experiences and discuss meaningful subjects that are often thought about but seldom expressed. They needed a space where they would share, learn, and grow; where they could exercise their minds and hearts instead of being merely entertained and occupied.

Our Sharing Group was born. It began over a year ago with a small group of women, aged sixty-two and older (except for me—I was twenty-five). Once a month we met to discuss meaningful, stimulating subjects. Our first discussion: happiness. We talked about what brings happiness to our lives: health, family, nature, God, friendship, children. "Isn't it wonderful to be able to wake up in the morning, to walk outside and see the trees, the birds, and the sky? That makes me happy!" said one of our "life experts."

"I am happy to be healthy and alive."

"I am happy to have food and shelter."

"I am happy to have a family, to love, to have loved, and to be loved."

"I am happy to know God."

"What makes me happy," said another lady, "is to go out there and feed the ducks by our lake" (our lake is a stopped-up retention pond). Everyone agreed to that, and we all laughed. The good feelings flowed, and the sharing grew.

Other topics followed: friendship, "why me?" unconditional love, changes, relationships, the road within, the miracle of me, nature, solitude, and death. We began the meetings with a short presentation, usually a reading, and lessons followed. What I had believed to be deep, difficult philosophies and concepts, these ladies knew intimately and had been applying throughout their lives. Profound feelings, thoughts, and experiences were expressed easily and fluently. Hearts opened. It was a gift to share and receive.

Our meeting on the topic of solitude was full of inner discovery. We talked about being alone and how it feels. We explored the differences between solitude and loneliness: "Loneliness is a feeling—you wallow in it. Solitude is a state of peace of mind and heart—you build on it."

"In loneliness, you forget the blessings, in solitude you remember them," commented Carlota, a perceptive and brilliant Spanish woman.

"Solitude is being at innermost peace."

"Solitude is necessary, for it leads to reflection and to a deeper understanding of our world and ourselves."

"In solitude we find and give our souls needed forgiveness, truth, and tranquility. With inner growth, you look for and appreciate solitude. Then you are no longer afraid to listen, really listen, to the voice within."

Our meeting about death was wonderful. I read an excerpt from Elisabeth Kübler-Ross. What I had thought might be a feared subject was actually a welcomed and spirited discussion. "I am not afraid to die anymore," said Jesse, a quiet Southern lady. "I realized, why should I fear death if I never feared life?"

A most precious gift came from Dorothy, a lively, loving seventy-five-year-old. She pulled out a newspaper clipping and said, "Look what I found in *Dear Abby*!"

*I am standing on the seashore. A ship spreads her sails to the morning breeze and starts for the ocean. I stand watching her until she fades on the horizon, and someone at my side says: "She is gone!" Gone where? The loss of sight is in me, not in her. Just at the moment when someone says, "She is gone," there are others who are watching her arrival. Other voices take up the glad shout: "Here she comes!" And that is dying.*

The lessons and the gifts have been many. I feel fortunate to have shared and to continue sharing with these wells of wisdom, depth, and beauty. I learned that there are truly no boundaries between human beings. We are all individuals, put together with the same parts but in different ways. I have met extraordinary people here. We have shared, learned, and grown together. I know that they appreciate having a time and a space where they can stop and think, where their life experiences and feelings are valued as an immense treasure—the biggest indeed. Sometimes they amaze me with their zest for life and honesty. In knowing many of these remarkable people, I recognize common denominators: endurance, openness, faith, gentleness, and most of all, love. Our differences in background, experience, age, and personality melt away, and the essence of our hearts unites in sharing. I wonder: What if I had hurriedly dismissed my visitor so that I could get my paperwork done? I am glad that I listened to that feeling deep inside.

The lessons and gifts are many, if only we are willing to receive them. A way to begin receiving is to stop and listen.

*Martha L. Name*
Seeds of Unfolding

Miracles happen. Not every day and not without effort, but miracles can and do happen to those who never give up!

# The Story of Emily

United Kingdom

≫ ≪

*Where there is great love, there are always wishes.*

## *Willa Cather*

After World War II, I worked in a refugee camp for children. The children had either been orphaned or separated from their families and were considered lost. By 1952, many of these children had been reunited with relatives and the ones that remained in the camp had little hope of ever returning to those who loved them. Day after day we searched for some tiny clue to their identity, anything that might help us identify them.

One girl, we guessed to be about thirteen, had been so traumatized during the war that she was mute. The child had been brought to the camp by a man who said he guessed the girl was British. In fact, no one really knew for sure. During the Occupation, she was passed from one family to another to avoid detection. She had been found in a hedgerow beside a road leading out of Paris when people were fleeing the city. She was known affectionately as *Herisson,* which translated means hedgehog or urchin; she would only respond to that name. She was assigned to me. Day after day we sat together, sometimes she'd reach over and cover my knees with her sole possession, a small tattered quilt that she carried with her everywhere.

One day, as I patted her quilt, I felt an unusual thickness between the two halves of a quilted square. Curious, I looked more closely and saw that the threads around this square were different from those used in the rest of the quilt. I pointed it out to Herisson, and asked if I might open the square. She nodded, "Yes." Carefully I removed the top layer of the quilting and pulled out a piece of fabric. Embroidered on it were the words:

> *For Emily, to keep you warm when we cannot,*
> *Love, your grandparents in Chester,*
> *John and Alice Scott.*

This was the beginning of Hedgehog's journey home.

One afternoon, in a little cottage in Chester, England, John and Alice Scott told me of the horror they experienced on that road leading out of Paris. German fighter planes machine-gunning the road, their son and daughter-in-law killed, and Emily lost in the confusion. They fled, and eventually escaped back to England. They recounted the intervening years. Sadly, John shook his head and told me that no amount of good works providing for other children healed the broken places he felt within. He mused, "I can't get her out of my mind . . . I just pray some-day, by some miracle." I interrupted, "How would you know her if you saw her now?" Alice looked at me, "Why, she had a little birthmark on the back of her neck, shaped like a butterfly." I knew the mark.

After reams of paperwork, little Hedgehog, quilt in one hand, mine clutched in the other, knocked on the door of the little cottage in Chester. The door flew open.

"Here is your little butterfly," I said. With tears flowing freely down his cheeks, John knelt down, looked her in the eye and said, "Oh Emily, for so long I prayed to be able to hold you once again." I heard Emily speak for the very first time, "I love you, Grandpa," as she wiped the old man's tears away with her tattered quilt.

*Reverend Michelle Woodhouse*

Connections happen between people. It could be a glance, a smile, a kindness, a moment of recognition, an unspoken bond. When a true connection is made, both people know it, feel it, and treasure it.

# The Doorman

France

⇒ ⇐

*Every time a man unburdens his heart to a stranger he reaffirms the love that unites humanity.*

### *Germaine Greer*

The year was 1945 and World War II in Europe had blessedly and finally ended. Thousands of young men were moved from the battlefields to Paris to await the day they would be sent home or to the Pacific to, once again, risk their lives.

They were scarred from the horrors they had seen and been a part of; kindness, quiet, and peace were the medicines necessary to heal their wounds, at least enough so they could pick up their guns once again.

My husband Gene was one of those men. Though he was decorated several times for bravery, war was foreign to his heart, so perhaps this was why he was particularly drawn to people of personal warmth.

He was billeted in the Hôtel Napolean, located at the heart of Paris. The elevator was a cage with pulley ropes and the rooms were clean but simple. There was a doorman. His job was to stand outside the hotel, open doors for guests and greet them. He would always say, *"Bienvenue á Paris"* and he treated every young serviceman as a special friend, almost like a son. He remembered their names and was not above hugging them from time to time. They had liberated his country and he loved them for it. His name was M. Jean Fratoni.

Thank God that the war ended in the Pacific before those men (boys) had to go. Instead they were sent home. When they left Paris and Hôtel Napolean, there were tearful good-byes with M. Fratoni.

Forty years later Gene wanted to run the Paris marathon on his sixtieth birthday, so we went to Europe. He had never returned since the war but finally, with my emotional support, he was ready to visit towns he'd helped to liberate, roads he'd walked while German soldiers were on the hills on either side of the road picking the American soldiers off like flies, cemeteries where so many of his buddies lay buried. It was a highly emotional time for us but the pinnacle was yet to come.

When we arrived in Paris, we went to an American-owned hotel to register for the upcoming marathon and we thought we'd probably stay there as so many of the runners were doing. But Gene had an idea.

"You know what? Let's find Hôtel Napolean and stay there." It sounded good to me if it was, indeed, still there. In 1945, it was a simple hotel, sort of the no-frills variety, so when we, found it, after asking directions, it was nothing like we expected. Hôtel Napolean had become one of the finest, most elegant hotels in all of Paris.

"Oh boy, it's nothing like it was and anyway, I'm sure it is very expensive." Gene said this softly, but there was something in his voice and heart that made me realize how touched he was just being there.

Listening to my heart, I said, "Oh, but it's so beautiful and to think, you stayed in this very place forty years ago. Let's at least check it out."

We pulled the car up to the curb next to the hotel. For some reason neither of us moved when suddenly Gene drew in a breath and whispered, "Ohhhhh."

I watched as a very old gentleman bowed and opened Gene's door. *"Bienvenue á Paris,"* he said. Gene seemed suspended in time as he stared at the man. Finally he stepped out of the car and stood facing the man.

I saw tears well up in Gene's eyes as he placed his hands on the man's stooped shoulders. Swallowing hard, he said simply, "You were here during World War II, weren't you?" The man nodded holding his body very still. Gene continued, "So was I. I was one of the soldiers who lived at the Hôtel Napolean and you were so kind to me. My name is Brody."

The old gentleman searched Gene's face and then threw up his hands and, with trembling arms, he enfolded my husband, repeating over and over, *"Je me rappelle, cher ami.* I remember."

The two men stood in the street together, each recalling a very different time and circumstance and who somehow, after forty years, recognized each other.

Finally, they gathered up the baggage at M. Frantoni's insistence. We knew it was very expensive but they found a tiny room with a bath that we felt we could afford. While we were showing credit cards, M. Frantoni left us to speak briefly to an official-looking man. When we

were taken to our room, it was not the "least room in the inn" but rather
an elegant suite with antique furniture and priceless rugs. When we said
there was some mistake, Gene's friend from so long ago just smiled and
said, *"Seulement le mieux pour vous"* (only the best for you).

***Jean Brody***

Things are the way they are until they aren't. It takes strong people to change cultural norms. It takes listening and honoring your inner reality. Mollie found herself in a situation that was unacceptable to her. She found the strength and courage to change her life. Her story reminds us that all things are possible.

## Against All Odds

Ethiopia

⇒ ⇐

*Success is to be measured not so much by the position that one has reached in life as by the obstacles which he has overcome.*

### Booker T. Washington

"I am not here to be rich and collect every penny. I am stubborn. I don't lie. I don't cheat. I follow my heart and I don't compromise," she says. But this is a small part of Mollie's story. Mollie has defied convention and challenged authority all her life—except when it comes to authentic Italian food, an art she reveres. "I never give up," says Mollie, her dark eyes shining. "No one can hold you. No one can stop you from becoming. No one!"

Mollie was raised with four brothers and four sisters in the Tigre province of Ethiopia. Her mother was a homemaker and her father was a successful businessman who was determined that his daughters were also to be well-educated—an unconventional idea in Islamic society. Mollie's father was criticized at the mosque for those beliefs. The family was upper class, and Mollie's parents arranged her marriage to a man twice her age. At fourteen, she became a bride.

In Islamic society, women are to obey their parents and husbands. Mollie's wishes for independence and freedom were considered shameful. Not only that, but Mollie was pregnant. "One night," she explained, "I didn't want him [her husband]. I said, 'I don't want this' and I cried. I moved in with my parents and I asked for a divorce. The Islamic court did not want to give it to me. So I told them, 'If you don't give it to me I will convert to Christianity.' They said, 'You bluff. You threaten. Islamic society favors the man.' I did not give up. Two years later, I finally got my divorce."

Mollie had a son, Ali, whom she gave to her parents to raise, a cultural tradition with the firstborn. At sixteen, Mollie moved to Addis Ababa, the nation's capital, to live with her oldest brother and to attend school. There her life changed. "I wanted to do things like the Christians—they had so much freedom. Women did not have to cover up [in traditional clothing]. They drove cars and went dancing. I wanted to be independent like them." When her father would visit, she could not accompany him to the mosque because she had humiliated him . . . by wearing lipstick! Mollie was banished from her brother's house for her Western lifestyle. Her family shunned her. Although they loved her, they could not understand her behavior. She was regarded as "uncontrollable."

"My brother was told to kidnap me and bring me home so that I could be punished," Mollie says. "The king kills his daughters in my culture."

Mollie, thank goodness, was never kidnapped. Instead, she started a photography business and drove a Fiat around the capital. Ultimately, her family became impressed with her business acumen and loaned her money to open a camera shop. "I was rebellious, like a butterfly. I did everything. It was shocking to Islamic people. I was condemned. My behavior was unacceptable."

Mollie did well with her camera store, and in time, her son came to live with her. But Mollie became concerned with a deformity in Ali's hip. Ethiopian health care was mediocre, so Mollie decided to leave the country to find better medical care for her son. Rex Fleming, then a faculty member at Brooks Institute of Photography, was shooting commercials for Ethiopian airlines at the time and met Mollie while buying film at her store. Mollie believed if she could get out of Ethiopia, she could somehow make arrangements for Ali to join her. Fleming offered Mollie a one-year scholarship to Brooks, and she accepted.

"I had to bribe everybody to get out of the country," she recalls. "It was very difficult; however, I didn't give up. If I start something, I finish it." In 1980, Mollie left her twelve-year-old son with her brother and went to Rome to visit friends. She then traveled on to the United States. She was twenty-six.

A year after arriving in California, Mollie sent for Ali, who underwent a series of surgeries. Walking to her job at the Hallmark store, Mollie passed a tall businessman. She noticed that he did not take his eyes off of her. "I saw him in the parking lot and I knew in my heart that he would find me," she says. Robert Ahlstrand was "pretending to be interested in some things for his CPA business." She recalls, smiling, "He gave me his card and took my phone number. And we met." They were married eight months later.

"I loved him the first moment I saw him," she says tenderly. "I love him. He is a wonderful husband." Mollie worked as a bank teller and attended UCSB to study political science. To continue her studies, she needed to be fluent in one more language. She returned to Rome, her favorite city, to visit friends and brush up on her Italian. The year was 1988, and Mollie had been married for five years.

In Rome, she had an epiphany. She phoned her husband. "I told him I wanted to stay in Italy and study to become a chef," she recalls, seemingly unaware that such an announcement would upset most husbands. Ahlstrand reassured his wife and then flew to Rome to see her. "You were meant to be a chef," Ahlstrand told his wife. "Learn everything you can. We will sacrifice now, and when you come back, we will open a restaurant and live happily."

Mollie believes she has succeeded throughout her life because she never gave up, never stopped striving. She scoffs at the thought of being hindered because of her gender or race. "Look at me," she says, gesturing to her face and body. "I am black, Ethiopian, Muslim, and a woman. No one held me back. No one can hold you. If you want, you can go to space. You can be an astronaut. You can. Or you can be a chef with a successful restaurant of your own!"

*Mollie Ahlstrand*

RULE **4** FOUR

# A Lesson Is Repeated Until Learned

*Lessons will be repeated to you in various forms until you have learned them. When you have learned them, you can go on to the next lesson.*

In order to change, you must first know where you are and then find out where you want to end up. Sometimes circumstances seem overwhelming. It is in those moments that vision, purpose, and perseverance really matter. Whenever family members are reunited, regardless of their nationality, race, or creed, the result is overwhelming gratitude. Phyllis E. Johnson allows us to peek into a world that may be remote geographically, but is within each one of our hearts.

## You Don't Need Words

Serbia

➣ ➢

*The soul of a journey is liberty, perfect liberty, to think, feel, do just as one pleases.*

### *William Hazlitt*

Today we are taking an elderly woman to meet her daughter. A common enough occurrence, but at noon, under the harsh Macedonian sun, the woman walks through endless acres of white canvas tents on a field of crushed stone. She has with her all of her worldly belongings. It isn't much to carry; everything fits into one partially filled black plastic garbage bag. We help her into the four-wheel-drive vehicle we use on the dusty, unpaved country roads, and head for the camp gates. The objective of the journey is a reunion with her daughter. There are forms to be filled out, and permissions to be obtained to transfer from one refugee camp to another. As we stop at the guardhouse, the Macedonian police are obvious about the fact that they don't like the look of our papers, nor are they pleased that we don't have a copy to give them. They have never asked for a copy before; however, today they clearly want one, and we don't have it. As Besim, our interpreter/friend, negotiates with them, the elderly woman looks outside at the men shouting and waving their hands. The tears fill her eyes and her hands cover her face. She fully expects any minute to be forced from the vehicle and told that she can't leave. The fear of once again anticipating never seeing her daughter alive is too much for her to bear. She begins muttering to herself quietly and I can barely make out the word "Allah" repeated over and over again.

Finally a deal is struck with the guard; a promise is made to bring him the required papers tomorrow and we are allowed to pass. A deep breath is taken by all who are in the car. As we bump and bounce along the dusty road, we pass fields of poppies, purple thistle, and horse-drawn hay wagons. Towering over all, the mountains surrounding us hold up a canopy of cloud cover.

It is evident that the elderly woman has put on her best clothes for the reunion. She is wearing an ankle-length striped skirt, and what appears to be her best gray scarf covering her hair and trailing down her back. A friend has loaned her a little lipstick to add color to her face. Her weathered and lined face is aglow with anticipation.

We stop at a mineral spring to get some water, and while the men are out of the truck, she begins to describe to me what happened to her. I can't understand one word she says, but her desire to communicate is so strong that she shows me with her gestures. She removes one of her stockings and points to the huge blisters on her feet. She holds an invisible machine gun in her arms, and moves it from side to side in a wide arc. She mimes a knife, slashing at her arms and torso, as tears flow down her cheeks. I feel glad that I don't understand more of the words she says; I'm not sure I could keep my composure if I did. Perhaps understanding the words might make it easier, focusing on familiar sounds rather than the raw pain and horror; I'm not sure. My throat is too tight, and my eyes too blurred with tears to sort out the truth.

When we pull into the gates of the Bojane camp, there are more tears, but this time they are different. As the daughter approaches our vehicle, the mother is overcome with emotion. As mother and daughter embrace, they kiss each other's faces hundreds of times. They gently stroke each other's cheeks as confirmation that they are not dreaming. These are the faces they both feared they would never see again. Both mother and daughter escaped from Kosovo, and neither knew whether the other was alive or dead.

They thank us profusely, and ask Allah to protect us and our work. We reply that we are happy to help; and we are. These are the moments that make the hot tents, the scorching sun, the strange food, and lumpy beds worth it.

We have fulfilled our mission. This is why we are here: healing the pain of war through connections, one loved one reunited with another.

*Phyllis E. Johnson*

Courage is doing the right thing, especially when you're afraid. The only good things about war are the moments when people transcend their differences and connect at the human level. It shows that the higher self is present even when fear permeates the air. William T. Moore shares with us his story of courage to give us hope that someday we will be able to live without war.

# The Eleventh of August

United States

≫ ≪

*The story of love is not important—what is important is that one is capable of love. It is perhaps the only glimpse we are permitted of eternity.*

### *Helen Hayes*

Though this story recounts events that took place in the middle of a war, it is not a war story. It is instead a testimonial of extraordinary courage, the courage of an anonymous lady who listened to her heart and made a difference.

In 1969, I was a U.S. Army lieutenant serving as an advisor with one of the infantry battalions of the South Vietnamese Army. On the afternoon of August 11, I was aboard a helicopter flying above the Mekong Delta, accompanied by Captain Tung, the commander of the battalion, and my assistant, a brave and very capable young sergeant named Ken. We were surveying the terrain in preparation for an aerial insertion of our battalion, some four hundred men in all.

Suddenly, one of the small observation helicopters on the mission with us came under automatic weapons fire. Following the tracers, we easily pinpoint where the fire had come from—a hut on the edge of a clearing almost directly below us.

"Permission to bust the hooch," the pilot of an accompanying Cobra gunship requested of one of our pilots, the aircraft commander (AC). That was routine language for opening fire on the sniper and his hut. The AC at once passed on the request to the command group—Captain Tung, Ken, and me—but it was a mere formality. They expected that we would, of course, want the Cobra to fire back.

Yet something made us pause before approving the strike. A few yards in front of the hut below, we could see what appeared to be a woman standing stock-still. Surely she knew an automatic weapon had just been fired at a U.S. helicopter from her hut, and she must have known that the helicopter gunships accompanying us were then preparing to bring their awesome firepower to bear on the hut, quite likely killing her—yet still she didn't move. Something wasn't right.

"Negative, permission denied," we responded. It would be an understatement to say that our response didn't go over well with the AC or the rest of the helicopter crew. After some heated words expressed in frustration and disbelief, he asked angrily, "What are your intentions?"

I'm not sure we honestly knew our intentions at that instant, but faking conviction, I ordered the AC to land the chopper so we could get out and investigate. Another heated discussion followed, this time including a lecture about aircraft safety and pilot responsibilities. I'll skip the details and the profanity and simply say that the pilot did land, close to the hut, and the three of us jumped out.

We advanced cautiously to say the least. Even at that late moment I don't think it was clear to any of us exactly what we should do next. But we kept moving and fired a few rounds over the hut as we maneuvered closer. When we approached the woman, it was obvious she was petrified, her knuckles white as she grasped her rake. She didn't move or acknowledge us, but we could see tears streaming down her cheeks. We brushed by her and took positions outside the front entrance.

Inside the hut we could see the familiar sight of an earthen bunker, common in Vietnamese farmhouses during the war. We knew it might contain at least one enemy soldier armed with an automatic weapon. Standard routine would be to throw in a grenade and let him run out or die in the blast. But nothing about this was routine. I'm not sure we could have explained it at the time, but killing the enemy just wasn't our aim in this instance. Though we didn't speak, our next move became apparent when we realized that none of us was going to pull a grenade. Somehow this encounter was meant to end differently.

The time had come for us to do something decisive. Glancing back once more at the immobile woman in the clearing, I hunched down to crawl inside the bunker with my .45 drawn. I stooped into the pitch-dark entrance, but before I got completely inside, I collided with someone.

Scared out of my wits, I shouted loud enough to wake the dead. The young man with whom I had collided must have been as frightened as I was. I held my .45 in his face and backed out of the bunker with him in tow. As he emerged into the sunlight, we saw he was only about eighteen years old. He was our Viet Cong sniper, as his weapon and ammunition testified, yet he offered no resistance as Ken quickly gathered these things up and steered him toward our waiting chopper.

On our way, we passed the woman again. She had not moved, but the tears no longer flowed, and her face showed relief. The relief on the boy's face eerily mirrored hers, not only in expression but in feature and line. I think by then we had all realized the very special nature of this event.

Tension dissipated like the lifting fog with the understanding of what her courageous stand had led us to do. And for a few fleeting moments, we celebrated, right there in the middle of a combat zone—warriors who had been moved to commit an act of kindness by the supremely heroic act of a desperate lady. As the chopper crew helped us load up the prisoner, these same men who had so sharply opposed our maneuver smiled and shook our hands. Even the AC reached out his door to shake our hands as Captain Tung playfully messed up the boy's hair.

As we lifted away from the clearing, I gazed back down at the woman. She still hadn't moved, but her gentle eyes and subdued smile said more clearly than words ever could:

Thank you for sparing my son.

*Dr. William T. Moore*

Animals play an important role in our lives. Since they communicate without words, animals can connect with our core essence. Jack Lovick shares with us his miraculous story of his connection with a horse. If you have a special relationship with a cat, dog, bird, or horse, you will understand what Jack experienced.

# Horses as Healers

Australia

*In the important decisions of personal life, we should be governed, I think, by the deep inner needs of our nature.*

### Sigmund Freud

I have always loved horses. Even as a child my passion for the smelly, four-legged creatures was unbridled. I couldn't imagine a day without the joy of throwing a leg over my horse and setting off into the country for a brisk ride.

One hot summer day in '72, I was out running an errand, when all of a sudden I felt dizzy and sick to my stomach. As I struggled to remain standing, I lost my balance and fell. Each time I tried to stand up, I fell again. I struggled to regain control, and had no idea what was wrong with me.

I made it all the way to my car, mostly crawling on my belly, opened the door and forced my heavy body into the driver's seat. I started the engine with the intent of going home, and found that I couldn't lift my leg to depress the clutch. When I tried to reach down and lift my leg, I realized that my left arm was useless as well.

With my left side virtually numb, I somehow managed to make it home. I pulled up to my house, turned off the engine, opened the door and promptly fell out of the vehicle onto the pavement and lost consciousness. The next thing I knew, I was being airlifted to a hospital in Melbourne. Through a foggy state, I could hear the hustle and bustle of the paramedics and my family crying.

Four days of my life were deleted, and when I finally awoke, I found myself in a hospital bed in Melbourne. I could see in the faces of my family and friends that things were not going well. I was soon informed that I had suffered a massive stroke and would be partially paralyzed; my life would be drastically changed, and I would never ride again. I was devastated.

After weeks of grueling physical therapy, I returned home and was able to walk with the assistance of a cane, but was still strictly forbidden to return to my passion. My heart lurched as I gazed at my beautiful horses grazing near the barn. Slowly my oldest stallion trotted over to me and nuzzled his nose against my cheek. I buried my face into his thick neck and gently stroked his velvet coat. It was truly more than I could take.

I called out to my youngest son Danny who was playing near the barn. I instructed him to bring me Bluebook's bridle and saddle. With a puzzled expression, he fulfilled my request and watched anxiously as I saddled the horse. "But Daddy, the doctor said you aren't supposed to ride." I put down my cane and with my good arm, struggled to mount the horse. After a few frustrating failures, I took a deep breath, closed my eyes, and suddenly heard a voice in my mind say, "You are going to be all right." At that moment I knew it was true. This time, with all my might, I managed to successfully mount the horse, and began circling the barn. With every step, my muscle memory became stronger and stronger. Just then my wife came running out of the house yelling for me to stop. Yet as she looked at me, tears began rolling down her cheeks when she saw how happy I was.

Every doctor that saw me claimed my riding days were over. I proved them wrong. I realized that day, thirty years ago, that with the power of passion, anything is possible. It's true, you really can fall in love with horses.

*Jack Lovick*

Love is never to be taken for granted. When you find your love, you can take it in stride, leave it to chance, or seize the moment and treasure it for all time. Michelle Constanescu shares her story, one that, if left to chance, would have ended quite differently. She chose to stop the repetition of her pattern and take charge of her life and her love.

# Romanian Rainbows

Romania

≫ ≪

*It does not take much strength to do things, but it requires
great strength to decide on what to do.*

### Elbert Hubbard

In the fall of 1993, I traveled to Bucharest, Romania, as a missionary's assistant. I had never left my country before, and I was looking forward to spending a month helping my missionary friend. But shortly after our arrival, Patricia injured her back, and had to stay in bed for ten days. As I had nothing to do, and was in a foreign country for the first time, she convinced me to call her twenty-five-year-old translator, a young man who had become like a son to her, and ask him to show me around the city. After ten days, we fell in love, but never revealed our true feelings. I returned to the States with a broken heart. I was certain we'd never see one another again.

About six months later while praying, I got the overwhelming intuition that I would someday marry this man. It felt like a message from above. I was so certain about this premonition that I stopped dating altogether and decided to wait for him. I didn't understand how we would ever see each other; however, two years later I was invited to return to Bucharest, this time with my friend and her husband.

By the end of the month in Romania, such a strong friendship developed between this man and me that I was certain I would marry him. Yet there were no signs of romance. Three days before I was scheduled to return home, I spent the evening praying that the following day would be "extraordinary." We were supposed to spend the entire next day together, just the two of us. I knew it was our last chance to be together before I returned to my homeland. Since we would be spending our time walking around the city, I prayed that God would provide the perfect weather for that particular day.

Imagine my surprise when I awoke the following morning to find the ground covered in wet, sloppy snow! It had been snowing and raining the previous night, leaving huge slushy puddles on the streets. I laughed to think that this was God's idea of perfect weather. I knew intuitively something special was going to happen.

As planned, the man I loved came to pick me up and we set out for our walk under a huge umbrella everyone affectionately called the "tent." I had only tennis shoes on, and it wasn't long before I was soaked up to my knees. Both of us were cold, wet, laughing, and enjoying each other's company. We decided to go back to the apartment where he lived with his mother and make some Jell-O I had packed at the last minute. He had never eaten Jell-O, and we thought it would be a fun alternative to staying out in the puddle-filled streets.

My Romanian friend used the Jell-O opportunity to thank me and give me a little kiss. This opened a flood of conversation and we finally admitted our true feelings for one another. The following day we were engaged, and two years later we were married in Bucharest.

At our wedding reception in the heat of July, the wind began to pick up, bringing with it a terrible thunderstorm. It began to hail, and all the guests stared out the windows at the torrents of rain. It ended almost as quickly as it had begun, and to everyone's surprise, above the tops of the buildings appeared a beautiful double rainbow. My new husband and I looked at it as a heavenly sign to the two of us that we had done the right thing.

We knew that we would be spending the rest of our lives enjoying one another, weathering storms, and always looking for the rainbows. No day was ever so special!

*Michelle Constanescu*

Believing in a higher power humbles us. Acknowledging that we require help from a source that we cannot see opens the door for unlimited possibilities. Asking for something means that we are human and wish for more than we currently have. Asking for blessings for others in need unites our energy in a common purpose. Giselle Tonee shares her uncommon story of the power of prayer.

# The Power of Prayer

Australia

⋙ ⋘

*In the life of the Indian there was only one inevitable duty—the duty of prayer—the daily recognition of the Unseen and Eternal.*

### Obiyesa of the Satee Dakotas

My second son was born exactly twenty years after my first. While I lay in the hospital room holding my baby, I heard an emergency call over the public address system: "A 311 on level four, room twenty-two." It rang out loud and clear. The nurses in my room became instantly mysteriously silent.

"What does that mean?" I inquired.

"Either a mother or child is in critical life-threatening condition. Whenever we hear a 311 call, all the staff stop whatever they are doing and pray. We believe that if we send all our energy and support to those dealing with the situation and we send love to the patient that truly miraculous things can and do happen." I listened in complete astonishment.

I had never heard of this kind of prescription. I had never seen a hospital that used love and energy as healing tools. Tears welled up in my eyes and bathed my face. I gazed at my beautiful son and gave thanks for his health. For that mother and infant who were in danger, I can't imagine any more effective medicine than prayer, positive energy, and love.

*Giselle Tonee*

We are all presented with choices. We can treat each other with kindness or with cruelty. We can turn our back or reach out. We can dominate and control or we can empower and liberate each other. Desmond Tutu shares how light emerged from darkness to illuminate behaviors that should never be repeated.

# No Future without Forgiveness

South Africa

➤ ⫷

*Surround yourself with only people who are going to lift you higher.*

### Oprah Winfrey

Our very first hearing was to be held in East London in April 1996. One other characteristic of the TRC that contrasted with other commissions elsewhere was its very public nature. In Chile the Truth Commission had conducted its work behind closed doors. Not so the TRC. Originally it had been suggested that the Amnesty Committee would do its work *in camera,* but the human rights NGOs agitated very strongly against this and their view prevailed, to give the TRC a feature that has been much admired by people of other countries. My colleagues had worked like beavers to get the show on the road so quickly. The logistics involved with the holding of a hearing were formidable. The statements had to be obtained and there was no guarantee that people would actually want to come forward. They might have been inhibited by intimidation not to blow the whistle on those who had abused them; they might refuse to be regarded as victims since they believed themselves to be combatants in a struggle; they might be disillusioned, not believing any longer that anything worthwhile could be expected from those who were forever making promises and being so painfully slow on delivery.

We need not have worried. As I have already indicated, we ended up obtaining over 20,000 statements. People quite extraordinarily did want to tell their stories. They had been silenced for so long, sidelined for decades, made invisible and anonymous by a vicious system of injustice and oppression. Many had been bottled up for too long, and when the chance came for them to tell their stories the floodgates were opened. We were distressed that not too many white people came forward. Those who did were quite remarkable persons, as we shall hear from one or two samples that I will describe.

We were anxious on other scores. The act was emphatic that the entire process has to be victim-friendly. This was one way in which the commission might fulfill that part of its mandate to help rehabilitate the civic and human dignity of those who came offering their hearts to the gaze of the world, exposing their most intimate anguish and pain. We were greatly privileged to be given that glimpse into the secret places of the souls of so many of our compatriots. I never cease to marvel, after these wonderful people had told their stories, that they looked so ordinary, so normal. They laughed, they conversed, they went about their daily lives looking to all the world to be normal, whole persons with not

a single concern in the world. And then you heard their stories and wondered how they had survived for so long when they had been carrying
such a heavy burden of grief and anguish, so quietly, unobtrusively, with
dignity and simplicity. How much we owe to them can never be com-
puted. Their resilience in the face of daunting challenges and harassment
that would have knocked the stuffing out of lesser mortals was in the
end quite breathtaking. These were men and women we had arrogantly
dismissed as "the ordinary people." In my theology there are no ordinary
people. Each one of us, because we are God's representative, God's
viceroy, God's stand-in, and a God-carrier—each one of us is a very special person, a VSP far more important and far more universal then your
normal VIP.

We owed to these people a great deal more than we will ever know or
be able to acknowledge. We had to ensure that they were really willing to
testify because they would in a sense become public property. There was
no way we could predict how the media and the public would react and
how they would treat those who were foolhardy enough to expose their
grief in public. We provided counseling to those who came to our offices
before what would be, even at the best of times, a grueling experience.

We provided them with people whom we called briefers, who accompanied the witnesses, sitting next to them as they testified, providing
them with comfort of their presence, passing a glass of water and the
ubiquitous TRC tissues to them when they broke down, as so many did
and so frequently. Some cynics disparagingly spoke of the Kleenex
Commission—because of the paper tissues we had available. We were
scrupulous about the seating arrangements. Pride of place was to be

reserved for the witnesses. We had to avoid any impression that they were in the dock, so they sat on the same level as the TRC panel hearing their testimony.

It was important that the witnesses should feel comfortable and at ease, hence the insistence that they were free to tell their story in the language of their choice. This meant that we had to provide simultaneous translation, and that is why the public image of the TRC included those who sat wearing headphones. That added to the complications of arranging for a hearing. The witnesses were also free to be accompanied by a relative who might sit with them as they testified. Arranging the transport, accommodation, and meals for all those who might attend a TRC hearing could be something of a logistical nightmare. My colleagues and TRC staff did a remarkable job in bringing this all off without too many hiccoughs, not just in the urban areas where venues and facilities were more easily available but also in the small towns and rural areas where they were often conspicuous by their absence.

The hearings were held in very different types of venues—town halls, civic centers, and especially church halls. The faith communities are to be very warmly commended for all they have done to facilitate this aspect of our work.

The TRC was not universally welcomed and popular. There were those who were passionately opposed, particularly those who felt the commission posed a threat to them, with the possibility of exposing their nefarious past, and those who had convinced themselves that it was really a smart ploy for engaging in a witch hunt against the Afrikaners.

We feared that they might very well want to sabotage the proceedings of the commission, hence security was an important issue. As it happened, our very first hearing was interrupted by a bomb scare. Proceedings had to be suspended while police dogs sniffed out the whole venue. Mercifully it turned out to be a hoax but we could not take chances, with the lives of so many at stake and with so much depending on a successful completion of our task. Those who were opposed to the process of reconciliation would have gloated at any mishap that befell the commission.

We wanted to ensure that people felt that they had had ample time to tell their story and that they had been duly acknowledged. As a result, the committee members who ran hearings were able to choose only a representative cross-section of witnesses to hear in any particular area. On average only one in ten of those who made statements was able to testify in a public hearing.

We might perhaps take it as a compliment that people came to regard the public hearing so highly. In large measure it was because the media played such a splendid role—radio, TV, the newspapers gave the TRC and its victim hearings (as they did the amnesty hearings) saturation coverage. When the SABC live radio broadcasts of the proceedings in the eleven official languages stopped for lack of funds, there was an outcry even from whites who hardly attended the hearings but who obviously were following them over the radio. We were given good advice by TV consultants from overseas on how to use TV cameras in the public hearings because most courts in many parts of the world do not permit live TV coverage of their proceedings. We were able to develop a policy for such coverage whereby the cameras were stationary and not obtrusive. Only the stills photographers complained because the requirement that they remain in one spot was too inhibiting and frustrating.

The atmosphere at our first hearing was solemn, though there were lighthearted moments later. We were going through an important ritual, too, the healing of our nation, and we could not be frivolous. Well, you could not be frivolous when you heard what had been happening to people. Our first hearing was going to be a crucial one; so much depended on our getting it right the first time, as this would impact on subsequent hearings positively or negatively as the case might be.

We were apprehensive. We held a deeply moving interfaith service in Mdantsane, a ghetto township near East London, the town where our first hearing was to be held. Asked by journalists how I felt on the eve of our first hearing, I said, "I certainly have very considerable butterflies in the pit of the tummy. But I also have a tingling sensation just being in this service, seeing so many people and the wonderful generosity of the people; that they do want this thing to succeed and that the stories must be told and that this process must end."

We prayed for God's blessings on our land, on the victims, the perpetrators, and the TRC. I always prayed in English, Xhosa, Sotho, and Afrikaans to underscore that the commission belonged to all. I welcomed all in these same languages for the same reason—to point up our diversity as a nation.

The City Hall was packed to the rafters—mainly with black people. The witnesses sat at a table facing the TRC panel and with their backs to the audience (a practice which we changed later). There were cubicles for the translators away on one side of the platform, and the hall was aglow with resplendent flowers and pot plants. Our police did a splendid job looking after security at the hearing, searching everybody at the security checkpoints.

As we filed in the audience rose to its feet and a deep hush fell over us all. I then went to shake the hands of those who were to testify at that four-day hearing, together with their relatives who had accompanied them. In silence I the lit a candle in memory of all who had died as a result of the conflict of the past. One of my colleagues read out a roll of honor commemorating all those who had fallen. And then we sang *"Lizalis' idinga lakho* (Let your will be done)" as we had sung it that day in Bishopscourt when Nelson Mandela and his ANC comrades met there on the day of his release from twenty-seven years in prison, and as it would be sung on countless other occasions of significance.

**Desmond Tutu**
No Future without Forgiveness

# RULE 5 FIVE

## LEARNING DOES NOT END

*There is no part of life that does not contain lessons. If you are alive, there are lessons to be learned.*

As each of us passes through our lives, the lessons continue. Some lessons are subtle and fleeting, while others are profound and forever life-altering. Zeroing in on those significant moments that changed our lives illumines not only the lesson but also enables us to experience our gratitude, no matter how difficult the situation was at the time. Diane Gloria Alegre-Pestano allows us to peek into a life-changing experience that was replete with life lessons.

## Boat Ride to Health

Philippines

≫ ≪

*I don't know what your destiny will be, but one thing I do know: the only ones among you who will be really happy are those who have sought and found how to serve.*

**Albert Schweitzer**

In 1993, I had just finished my schooling and had finally achieved my lifelong goal of becoming a licensed nurse. Excited about the work I was prepared to do, I became a missionary and volunteered for the Agape Rural Program. A female doctor, dentist, and I (all from Manila) were sent on our first assignment to the northern part of Palawan: Busuanga, very far from my hometown in Bulacan, near Manila.

We were involved in medical missions in the many islands in Busuanga where free consultations, medical and dental, as well as free prescriptions were dispensed. One day in December 1993, we headed to an isolated island called Cheey. Our task was to deliver medicine and help the people. Two boatmen and a midwife, natives of Palawan, who knew the islands, volunteered to accompany us on the journey. We all rode together in a tiny wooden motor boat.

The journey was about two hours' travel from Calauit. Just as we spotted Cheey, the motor on our boat gave out. The boatman tried in vain to bring the boat back to life. Finally he asked Nedi, our doctor, the tallest among us, to stand and wave something white in hopes that someone from the island might see it and rescue us. The two boatmen and the midwife exchanged glances and whispered among themselves. I wondered why these people, who were so attuned to the sea, would be acting so strangely when we were in such close proximity to the island.

We took turns waving the doctor's white shirt, but to no avail; no one from the island came to rescue us. The bamboo poles were too short to propel our boat and we had no oars or paddles. The anxiety in the tiny craft became infectious.

All of a sudden, someone started singing "Amazing Grace." One by one, we all joined in humming and singing hymns that reminded us of our individual faiths. Each person prayed to their respective God. We sat in the boat, enduring the heat, the salty air, and the nauseating rocking of our tiny, cramped boat. With uncertainty permeating the air, we continued singing and praying that we, who were serving our mission, would be delivered safely to do our work.

The boatman jabbed the bamboo pole into the water and miraculously hit sand. This broke the anxiety with a sigh of relief. Our singing ceased and we gave thanks for our deliverance. With the help of the waves it only took half an hour from that point to reach the shore.

We served two hundred people that day. We gave consultations, tooth extractions, health education, and much more. After supper that evening, while we were resting in the home of our host, I asked our boatman why he was so frightened during the whole event. His face broke into a gentle smile, "You see Diane, Cheey has one of the most dangerous tides in all the islands. Our boat stopped at the point where the big waves start; but we were actually scared of the sharp rocks on the shore nearby. One wave could have smashed our boat into hundreds of pieces if hurled against the rocks; many lives have been lost in exactly that same spot. This is the reason no one attempted to rescue us. When you saw me whispering . . . I whispered to my colleague that if the big waves came at that moment each of us was to take one of you with us and jump off the boat. You see . . . it was not my life that I was preparing to lose, but rather, your life that I was planning to save."

**_Diane Gloria Alegre-Pestano_**

Lessons may be difficult for young people to learn, yet they may also be just as challenging for older people to embrace. The real gift is for older people to somehow pass those lessons on to younger ones at the precise moment when they can really "get" them. It isn't always family members who can pass on this wisdom, sometimes it is a stranger who says the right thing at the right time. Joanna Slan shares such a precious moment.

## Seize the Moment

France

⇒ ⇐

*The moment you have in your heart this extraordinary thing called love and feel the depth, the delight, the ecstasy of it, you will discover that for you the world is transformed.*

### *J. Krishnamurti*

The thick cables strained, a low whine filled the air, and our elevator car lurched. Holding my son in my arms, I widened my stance to keep from falling. Unthinkingly, we looked up. We were climbing the Eiffel Tower, as one slow turn of the giant winch hauled us up above the clouds of Paris.

Across from me, an old woman scowled. Her expensive trenchcoat was buttoned up to her sagging throat, and a glorious shawl was pinned over one shoulder. In her manicured hands she held a designer purse, and she shifted herself wearily against the open grid of the elevator car, adjusting her weight against the carved head of a mahogany walking cane.

I had first noticed her in the Jules Verne restaurant, where we had eaten lunch. How out of place we seemed! The legendary cuisine of Jules Verne had attracted my husband and me, and since we were traveling *en famille,* we came with our two-year-old son. We savored each dish while juggling our busy tyke, in a dining room filled with international business people and elegant travelers from all over the globe. A phalanx of waiters, looking curiously like penguins in their tuxedos, retrieved flying spoons and sullied napkins as we struggled with our child at the table.

Alas! My fantasy had been to dine with my husband alone, here on the mezzanine of the Eiffel Tower, in my best black dress, sip champagne, and end the evening with a romantic toast to the sleeping City of Light. Finances and childcare, however, had not cooperated and I released my fantasy and stood here, holding a squirming infant and shrinking under the glare of an irritated matron. I could imagine that our frivolity had ruined her lunch. Bringing our child to this elegant environment must have been deemed totally inappropriate. Undoubtedly, she had judgments about "those ugly Americans!"

"How old is he?" Her gaze centered on my squirming son. I was taken aback. Her voice was low and smoldering with a cultured European accent.

"He is twenty-eight months old."

"Oh." She grunted and turned her head to view the plaza below us. Then she turned and lifted her cane to point at my child.

"Don't let him forget this day." She paused. "Some of us wait too long. My husband and I always said we'd come to Paris. But first it was the children. Then it was the business, and now . . ."

I leaned toward her. "Now?"

Her sagging eyes locked onto my son's. Hers were a faint shade of blue, like blueberry stains in a sink. His were as green and crisp as the grass below us. "Now, he is gone and I am here alone."

My husband shifted and pulled me close to him. My son giggled in delight.

"It's . . . hard to enjoy such beauty . . . alone." She sighed and wiped the back of her hand across her eyes as a small child would. Then she looked away.

"Seize the moment while you still have it. All too soon it slips through your fingers."

*Joanna Slan*

S tuff happens. What do you do when things happen that were unexpected, unintended, and unwanted? How you react, what you say, and ultimately what you do really makes the difference. In Luiz Alberto Py's story, we get to see up close something that happened and how he and his son handled it. An unforeseen lesson that turned into an incredible blessing.

# Alive and Well

Brazil

➤ ⬅

*Kindness can become its own motive.*
*We are made kind by being kind.*

### *Eric Hoffer*

It all began thirteen years ago when I was awakened in the middle of a Sunday night by the phone ringing. Someone told me my son had had a car accident and had suffered many fractures in his legs. He was eighteen years old. After two days, he developed a hospital infection in his compound fracture that then evolved into gangrene. Over four days, he underwent daily surgeries to remove dead tissue, always running the risk of having to have his leg amputated. Ten days after the accident, with the gangrene taken care of, he underwent a new surgery for the fractures.

One of the worst problems with a critically ill patient is that improvements are usually very slow, whereas setbacks are sudden and violent. The new surgery caused an infection in the blood (septicemia), which almost killed him. André—his brain numbed by the infection—wrenched off the intravenous lines four times. He tried to get up from the bed saying he wanted to leave, he couldn't stand the pain any longer. He had to be tied down. It is terrible to see a son in this condition, but only my presence would calm him down. He pleaded to be let loose. I untied one of his hands and held it. He became calmer, drifting between consciousness and sleep, as he held my hand tightly. I told myself I had to make the most of that contact: I didn't know how long I'd still have the chance to have André alive, with me. Any movement of his fingers meant my son was still communicating with me, even if it was only to tell me how he was suffering.

On the following day, André showed some improvement, but his life was still at risk. Exhausted after a sleepless night, I went home, lay down, and cried. After some time, I managed to say out loud what my heart was feeling: "My little boy is suffering, I don't want to lose my son, I want him alive and well, oh God!" I'm not a religious person, but I believe there is something beyond our knowledge, something we glimpse sometimes. In my despair, I felt that I had to make a commitment to God so that André could survive. Something Jesus Christ said sprang to mind: "Many are called upon, but few are chosen." There was my answer: to place my capabilities and qualities at His service. I prayed that He might exchange André's life for mine, my wish to dedicate my life to His Will. At that moment, I felt great peace of mind, I was almost sure that everything André needed in order to get well had been done and that from then on things would get better. I felt our fate was in His hands and that I would accept everything that was forthcoming with serenity.

Little by little, André started recovering. His will to concentrate on the future and forget the past was incredible. He would often talk of the day when he would be able to sit in a wheelchair; later, he would dream of his crutches he would use and the progress he would make. However, on one occasion he said, "Dad, the accident could have been avoided." I felt a sudden inspiration and a voice that came from me replied, "André, I admire your ability to face the future with optimism and not waste time looking back. We can't change what happened, there's no point in suffering by believing things could have been different, because they weren't. The important thing is to look ahead to the future and think about the best we can do for ourselves." After this day, I never heard him regret the accident again. If anything troubled him, he was able to avert it. I admired his stoicism, the courage and maturity with which André faced his torment and that led me to believe he would become an upright person, someone who knows how to make the most of life. During his stay at the hospital, he kept his spirits high, he was even happy. He was determined to get better and all this contributed a great deal to overcoming that brutal accident. After four months, he left the hospital and, a little over a year later, he was walking again.

As a result of the gangrene, André lost the whole outer side of his left leg: the fibula, arteries, nerves, all the muscles and the ankle joints. Nevertheless, despite the small handicap in walking and running, he was able to move on in his profession and even get a job abroad. André has lived in London for over ten years as a photojournalist. Last September, I visited him. He had just undergone surgery to amputate his left leg just below the knee, one more step in the long process that had begun thirteen years ago. His doctors suggested he undergo surgery because, besides the sequela, he had developed chronic ostemyelitis (bone infection) in the leg. The infection had appeared several times and on five occasions he'd had to be hospitalized. André saw the amputation as an opportunity to improve his life quality. "I'll be able to play soccer again," he said, with excitement, when I visited him at the hospital after the surgery. He talked to me with joy about his plans for becoming a paraolympic athlete. On seeing him so full of optimism, I am sure God has kept His part of our deal marvelously well. I have tried hard to keep mine.

I believe I'll be with my son in Athens in 2004.

*Luiz Alberto Py*

Love transcends borders, genders, race, and religion. Love is the universal connector of all humans. A mother's love is also universal. Mothers don't start wars because they know what it takes to grow, nurture, and develop a person. After all the care, effort, and giving, it is unthinkable to sever that life prematurely. Eri Adrian shares with us an example of "A Mother's Love."

# A Mother's Love

Indonesia

⋙ ⋘

*Love that lasts involves a real and genuine concern for others as persons, for their values as they feel them, for their development and growth.*

**Evelyn Duvall**

For Ita, raising her daughter by herself was all but impossible. A traumatic accident caused her to lose the functionality of both her feet. Another tragic moment followed when her husband left her. She had to make ends meet by getting a job at a printing factory located in the middle of Jakarta, which was operated by handicapped people. Fortunately, accommodations were provided for her and her daughter, just around the corner from the print shop.

Due to the economic turmoil throughout Indonesia, the factory owner had to cease operations. The employees were given a choice. They could either leave with no compensation, or stay with the hope that the factory might someday reopen. Ita and her daughter decided to stay even though she knew the only way to feed and educate her daughter was from generosity from kind-hearted people.

Ita had been paralyzed and used a wheelchair for many years; however, she never gave up hope. She had one dream and one dream only. That was for her daughter to finish high school and to become self-supporting.

In Jakarta, I had the privilege to meet Ita. At Health Day, eight doctors volunteered to check three hundred handicapped children and their families. Ita took the risk of calling me over to talk. She shared how this event had made a significant difference for her. As she trusted me, she continued to share what a struggle life had been.

I listened with my ears, my eyes, and my heart. After this intense conversation, I realized that being a mother means providing unconditional love to your child. Mothers sacrifice when they decide to have a child. A good mother will do anything to raise her child including doing everything by yourself.

My heart was touched; a mother's love never dies.

*Eri Adrian*

Preconceived notions often eclipse the present reality. It will sometimes take an extraordinary experience to open our eyes and let us see the truth. Blair P. Grubb shares with us his own awakening. It took but a moment, but for him, it will last a lifetime.

# Awakening

Germany

➣ ∈

*Love does not care to define and I am never in a hurry to do so.*

**Charles Du Bos**

There were so many admissions that night that I had begun to lose count—and my temper. A seasoned intern, I had learned well the art of the quick, efficient workup. Shortcutting had become a way of life. Morning was coming and, with it, my day off. All I wanted was to be done. My beeper sounded. I answered it. I heard the tired voice of my resident say, "Another hit, some ninety-year-old goner with cancer." Swearing under my breath, I headed to the room. An elderly man sat quietly in his bed. Acting put upon, I abruptly launched into my programmed litany of questions, not really expecting much in the way of answers. To my surprise, his voice was clear and full and his answers were articulate and concise. In the midst of my memorized review of systems, I asked if he had ever lived or worked outside the country.

"Yes," he replied. "I lived in Europe for seven years after the war." Surprised by his answer, I inquired if he had been a soldier there.

"No," he said, "I was a lawyer. I was one of the prosecuting attorneys at the Nuremberg trials." My pen hit the floor. I blinked.

"The Nuremberg trials?" He nodded, stating that he later remained in Europe to help rebuild the German legal system.

"Right," I thought to myself. "Some old man's delusion." My beeper went off twice. I finished the examination quickly, hurried off to morning sign-out, and handed over the beeper.

Officially free, I started out the door, but suddenly paused, remembering the old man, his voice, his eyes. I walked over to the phone and called my brother, a law student, who was taking a course on legal history. I asked him if the man's name appeared in any of his books. After a few minutes his voice returned.

"Actually, it says here that he was one of the prosecution's leading attorneys at the Nuremberg trials." I don't remember making my way back to his room, but I know I felt humbled, small, and insignificant. I knocked. When he bid me enter, I sat in the very seat I had occupied a short time before and quietly said, "Sir, if you would not mind, I am off duty now and would very much like to hear about Nuremberg and what you did there. And I apologize for having been so curt with you previously." He smiled, staring at me.

"No, I don't mind." Slowly, with great effort at times, he told me of the immense wreckage of Europe, the untold human suffering of the war. He spoke of the camps, those immense factories of death, the sight of the piles of bodies that made him retch. The trials, the bargaining, the punishments. He said that the war criminals themselves had been a sorry-looking bunch. Aside from the rude awakening of having lost the war, they could not quite understand the significance of the court's quiet and determined justice or the prosecution's hard work and thorough attention to detail. The Nazis had never done things that way. So moved had he been by the suffering he encountered there that he had stayed on to help build a system of laws that would prevent such atrocities from happening again. Like a child I sat, silent, drinking in every word. This was history before me. Four hours passed. I thanked him and shook his hand, and went home to sleep.

The next morning began early, and as usual I was busy. It was late before I could return to see the old man. When I did, his room was empty. He had died during the night.

I walked outside into the evening air and caught the smell of the spring flowers. I thought of the man and despair mixed with joy. Suddenly my life seemed richer and more meaningful, my patients more complex and mysterious than before. I realized that the beauty and horror of this world were mixed in a way that is sometimes beyond understanding. The man's effect on me did not end there. Despite the grueling call schedule, the overwhelming workload, and the emotional stress of internship, something had changed within me. I began to notice colors, shapes, and smells that added magic to everyday life. I learned that the gray-haired patients I had once called "goners" were people with stories to tell and things to teach. After nearly two decades, I still look to that night, remember that man, and reflect on the chance and privilege we have to share in the lives of others, if only we take the time to listen.

*Blair P. Grubb, M.D.*

Things aren't always as they appear. There are times when saying nothing is more helpful than interfering. Human kindness comes in many forms. Ichak Adizes shares his story of support that demonstrates the power of silence.

## Preserving Human Dignity

Albania

⇒ ⇐

*The greatest events—are not our noisiest, but our stillest hours.*

### *Friedrich Nietzsche*

I was born in Skoplje, Macedonia, a Sephardic Jew, a descendent of people who were expelled by the Spanish Inquisition in 1492. We were granted Spanish passports by the Spanish consul in Macedonia who was pleased to discover that we descended from the fiftenth century and even today, still spoke fifteenth-century Spanish.

When the Second World War broke out, all Macedonian Jews were herded into a concentration camp and sent to the gas chambers of Treblinka. My immediate family was released from the concentration camp because we possessed Spanish passports.

When we were released, we fled to Albania, which, at that time, was predominantly Moslem. We were not Moslems, but to avoid additional peril, we claimed to be. There is a term, "blood revenge," which means that lives must be sacrificed to atone for past slaughters. According to Moslem customs, those that flee "blood revenge" must be hidden. Therefore, the religious leader of Skadar hid us in a tiny village at the top of a mountain. There we were with no money, no electricity, no running water. We had escaped with barely our lives . . . but refugees without any resources would most likely perish.

Although my father had been forced to leave all our earthly possessions behind, he still possessed his wits. He thought long and hard about how he could manage to feed his family. Finally the idea came to him. He had always possessed a certain knowledge of hygiene, sanitation, and basic health. He managed to find some medical supplies, so he offered medical services to the people in exchange for food.

In order to appear unobtrusive in our new environment, we had to actively practice the Moslem religion, something which we knew nothing about. We were aware that our landlords, who were extremely religious, were watching our every move. I lived in fear that they would discover that we ate in hiding during Ramadan, a sacred feast, when all Moslems fast.

Eventually, the war came to an end. Our family survived by the grace of God. As my family was leaving the village, my father made a promise to return to the village one day to build the village a well. Fifty years after the war, in 1995, my father was finally able to return to fulfill our family promise.

It was a momentous occasion for everyone. The Israeli television crew captured it for the daily news. The village people were interviewed and asked if they had any idea that we were not practicing Moslems.

"Sure we knew," they said chuckling, "our religious leader told us they were Jews. They even ate during Ramadan."

The interviewer pressed, "Did you know whether the father of the family," he gestured to my father, "was a doctor?"

They laughed out loud, "Of course we knew. He was no doctor, everyone knew it, but that wasn't important. We took his 'medical services' and in exchange we gave them food so they could survive. We never said anything about it because the only thing we could give them was the right to their human dignity. It was the village secret. To live in peace and dignity in wartime means a lot."

**_Ichak Adizes_**

# RULE 6 SIX

## *THERE* IS NO BETTER THAN *HERE*

*When your "there" has become "here," you will simply obtain another "there" that will look better to you than your present "here."*

It is easy to get caught up in the "Here . . . There" syndrome . . . longing for a time in the future when things will be better than they are right now. It is a trap that presumes that things will be better than they are presently. This is not to say that you shouldn't have goals or pursue growth. The real challenge is to walk the dual-edge sword, having goals and continuing to grow while living in the present. Jan Toncar gives us a glimpse of real values and living in the present.

# The Difference Between Rich and Poor

Czech Republic

⇒ ⇐

*Always do right; this will gratify some people and astonish the rest.*

**Mark Twain**

My parents were born in Bohemia at the end of the last century. At the end of the First World War they moved to Korpvia, where my father started a small business working with his hands. Times were challenging and they struggled to make ends meet. With postwar problems including inflation, they had to resort to using all of their savings. I was born in 1919 and three years later my sister arrived. They were overjoyed to have their two little precious treasures, even though it meant stretching their already meager resources even further. Even though times were tough, they managed.

When I was eight years old, a short while before Christmas, our teacher asked us two questions: "Who among you do you consider to be poor? And who should qualify for a welfare council gift for Christmas?" She asked for a show of hands. All of those children who considered themselves to be "poor" raised their hands.

In a small town like ours, everybody knew each other. Not only did people know everyone by name, but they also knew where they lived, what they did, who they were related to, and how much money they had. After school our teacher asked me to come into her office. She sat me down and asked why I didn't raise my hand.

I said, "Because I'm not poor."

"And who, in your opinion, is poor?" she asked.

"Children who don't have any parents."

She stared at me in complete silence, and then she dismissed me.

The next day, my father returned from work, he had a huge smile on his face. I wondered what good fortune had come his way. I listened at the door as he described his good fortune to my mother.

He said that my teacher came to see him at his work. Then he said, "We should be very proud of our son." He told Mom what the teacher had said. That was the end of the discussion.

A few days before Christmas a parcel was delivered to our doorstep. We opened it on Christmas Eve. Before us lay two pairs of brand-new shiny shoes: one pair for my sister and one pair for me. We had never owned a pair of new shoes before.

I didn't know until many years later that that was our least abundant Christmas materially, but in our hearts we felt like the richest family in the world.

*Jan Toncar*

I t is not always easy to do the right thing. When you've set your heart on a dream, it can be very difficult to let go of it. Courage means doing the right things because you know in your heart that it is right. It all starts with one person who has the courage to stand up for what he or she believes in. Jane C. Willhite gives us her story about courage and integrity.

## I Choose to Stay Behind

Russia and United States

⇒ ⇐

*Watch your thoughts; they become words.*
*Watch your words; they become actions.*
*Watch your actions; they become habits.*
*Watch your habits; they become character.*
*Watch your character; it becomes your destiny.*

**Frank Outlaw**

Years ago, I was fortunate to be a part of a wonderful group called Youth Ambassador of America, a group whose mission is to take children ages thirteen through eighteen from all over the United States to meet with children from other countries. Once, there they would hold Youth Summit Conferences where groups from both countries would meet to discus peace relations. The trip that I was a part of was to escort fifty young people to the former USSR to meet with 150 Soviet young people.

I, along with my fifteen-year-old daughter and three other teenagers, whom we were bringing along with us, began our trip in San Francisco. The trip would take us first to Seattle, where we would meet the entire group, then to Helsinki, Finland, for group bonding and culture orientation, then Leningrad for sightseeing, and, lastly, to Moscow for the Youth Summit.

While in Leningrad we heard the wonderful news that the then-president of the USSR, Mikhail Gorbachev, would be meeting with our group in Moscow at the Kremlin. This news exceeded our expectations. To meet the leader who had changed the USSR so dramatically, and for him to personally show us the Kremlin, was awesome. The kids were thrilled.

Then came the bad news. Gorbachev would only see thirty members of our group. Our group numbered more that seventy including children, chaperones, and counselors. We learned that our then-President Reagan had just had a meeting with some visiting Russian children, and although the group was larger, our president had limited his meeting to thirty people as well. The limit placed on the numbers now seemed obvious.

We were all gathered in a large meeting hall in our hotel in Leningrad. I vividly remember what happened. The first reaction was, "We're not going if we all can't go." Then we heard, "Call him and demand that he see all of us." Then there were cries of anger, disappointment, and sadness. The kids were all talking at once, trying to come up with a solution. We adults hung back to let the children solve the problem. After realizing that this was the opportunity of a lifetime, what became clear to everyone was that if they all could not go, at least thirty would be able to experience this rare privilege.

Soon it was time to decide who the lucky thirty would be. For safety reasons it was decided that four of the thirty should be counselors. But who were the remaining twenty-six children? First it was that the oldest should go, then the youngest, then those that had been to Russia before. Should we take numbers, pick by chance? How do you decide who gets to go and who stays behind?

The children were faced with a life crisis, and reacted as we all do. There was arguing, fighting, crying, and withdrawing. This seemed to go on forever, but really it was not a very long time. In the midst of the chaos a loud voice was heard in the back of the crowd. As I looked back, I saw that the young man standing was Peter, one of the boys that I had brought on this trip. He stood and asked the crowd for attention. He had to speak many times, before the group quieted down. He began to speak, "My name is Peter, and I would love to meet President Gorbachev. And although I would really love this chance . . . I choose to stay behind." At that moment you could hear a pin drop in the hall. Everyone looked at him in amazement. There was quiet for some time, then another boy stood and said, "I also choose to stay behind." Children began to cry softly and look around. A girl stood, "I choose to stay behind," another stood, "I choose to stay behind." Then another and another, twelve, thirteen, seventeen had now stood and chosen to stay behind. Another stood holding hands with her friend and weeping as they held their heads high and said, "We choose to stay behind." Soon there were twenty-five, and then the last stood and said, "I choose to stay behind and I want all of you to go for all of us." Every person in the room was so moved by what had just happened that it took some time for anyone to move.

We began our Youth Summit right there in a hotel hall in Leningrad where we learned how to put someone else first and experience what happens when one truly becomes a "giver." We also learned that it truly only takes one to "make a difference."

*Jane C. Willhite*

It's not what you do, but the spirit in which you do it that matters. You bring your attitude with you to every situation and every task you encounter. You may not have a choice in life about your circumstances, but you always have a choice about your attitude. It is attitude that make the difference in every experience.

## It's All in Your Attitude

India

→ ←

*Minds are like parachutes—they only function when open.*

### *Thomas Dewar*

One day some friends and I visited some temples in India. At one site, a brand-new temple was under construction. There were only four laborers working on it. One of my friends approached one of the laborers. She asked him what he was doing. To this, he angrily replied, "Can't you see what I am doing?" His attitude showed his impatience with the question and his lack of enthusiasm for the task.

When the second laborer was asked the same question, he replied in a melancholic tone, "I am poor and need something to do to earn a living." His attitude showed that this activity was a means to an end.

The third laborer commented, "I am helping to build a temple." His attitude showed some pride in his affiliation with this project.

The fourth laborer's answer, however, was quite different from the others. He said, "I am helping to build a temple to honor God. I am blessed to be given the opportunity to help build this temple and to serve God in this manner."

All four laborers were doing the exact same work, on the same day, under the same hot sun. All of them were poor and uneducated; however, the way each one viewed their work was totally different. While the first laborer was disgusted with his lot, the fourth considered himself honored to be able to work in the service of God.

If everything we do is ultimately looked upon as a service to God, our attitude toward work will be different, and the quality of work must improve.

*Amisha Kanoria*

Some of us grumble at our circumstances when things don't go exactly the way we want them. Others make lemonade out of whatever lemons life happens to give them. Still others are grateful to have the opportunity to serve. Lilia Reyes Spindola shares a story that could go unnoticed were it not for her observation and willingness to share. It is an example of selfless giving with no agenda.

## Plates of Love

Mexico

➣ ⋘

*Things of the spirit differ from things material in that the
more you give the more you have.*

### *Christopher Morley*

The "Home of Our Lady of Charity" is located at 12 Limantitla Street, in Mexico City. It is dedicated to helping children with incurable diseases and those with severe mental illnesses. The majority of patients are bedridden due to the advanced nature of their condition. There are children of all ages, and the Franciscan sisters of the Immaculate Conception care for them. A few years ago I visited the house; the sisters received me with kindness and showed me the work they do in the home.

A sister accompanied me into the kitchen where the nuns were busily preparing lunch. In the midst of all the activity was a tiny woman who was moving about on a little cart made from a wooden board with sets of skateboard wheels attached to the bottom. This was her only means of ambulating since she had no legs. One of the sisters put a pot of rice on her little cart and handed her a spoon; she received it with an enormous grin and scurried off to serve the children. I asked the sister if the woman lived in the house, and, full of pride, she replied "No, the woman comes from her home every day to help serve lunch; her job is to fill each child's plate with spoonfuls of rice."

I was speechless. I took two plates and brought them to the woman so she could spoon rice on them. She smiled at me and said, "How nice that you have come to give us a hand, there is so much to be done." Her smile touched my soul. I bent over and hugged her, whispering, "Thank you." She lowered her eyes and with her sweet smile continued scooping rice onto the plates.

It wasn't just the rice that she gave those children each day; she filled each plate with spoonfuls of her love.

*Lilia Reyes Spindola*

It is easy to judge when people do not conform to our expectations and standards. Transcending judgments and finding generosity of spirit is the real challenge. Abdulhussain M. Tejani shares his experience of turning a judgment into an act of love.

## Thief in the Mosque

Tanzania

⇒ ⇐

*One can pay back the loan in gold, but one dies forever
in debt to those who are kind.*

**Malayan Proverb**

When my father was in his teens, his father took him to the mosque to pray. My grandfather, it seems, had a habit of keeping his loose change in his shirt pocket. As they prayed side by side, during one of the prostrations, the coins fell down onto the carpet.

Apparently deep in concentration, my grandfather did not notice. However, a gentleman seated nearby noticed the incident; the man reacted fast and scooped up the coins and went off into another corner of the mosque.

My father took everything in and as soon as my grandfather finished praying, he started to narrate what had transpired. My grandfather stopped my father from telling him who took the money.

He then proceeded to tell my father the following: "If this man has resorted to stealing inside the mosque, then it must be because his circumstances are really terrible. We must not be quick to judge such people."

Since our family owned a grocery store, my grandfather had an insight. Grandfather instructed my father to do a specific task every month. He said, "Every month, you create a parcel of all essential items required in a household and you send it to that man. Most important . . . is that you never let him know who sent it."

*Abdulhussain M. Tejani*

# RULE 7 SEVEN

## OTHERS ARE ONLY MIRRORS OF YOU

*You cannot love or hate something about another person unless it reflects something you love or hate about yourself.*

When someone behaves in a manner that doesn't match our own expectations, the result is often judgmental. Judgments can enable us feel superior to others. Neighbors have a tendency to notice each other and compare what they see. Regardless of the culture, people notice what is similar and what is different. When differences arise it is easier to point fingers rather than take responsibility for your actions. Astrid Stahlberg shares with us her personal experience of the "mirrors" in life and what she learned.

# Awful Neighbors

Sweden

≫ ≪

*Everything that irritates us about others can lead us to an understanding of ourselves.*

**Carl Gustav Jung**

We bought our home six years ago. The history of the land was interesting to us. Originally, the property was part of a large farm that held three separate buildings. The buildings were far enough apart to become the main houses for the surrounding land. Eventually, the farm was divided up and sold to three different families. We bought one parcel, and two couples who were very different from us bought the other two. The third couple, Arthur and Lynn, were traditional farmers, a generation older than we. We bought the final portion of the estate. When the others saw us, a young couple with two kids, John, eleven, and Sara, nine—soon to become teenagers—they were obviously less than pleased. I guess coming from different generations accentuated our differences. In addition, we didn't know the unwritten rules associated with the farm culture in this part of Sweden. It seemed like we started off on the wrong foot, and things just kept getting worse. We broke unwritten rules that we didn't even know existed. They looked down their noses at us, and we retaliated with righteous indignation. Finally we built a fence to distance ourselves from their judgmental eyes. Things went from bad to worse and the only contact between our family and theirs was hostility.

One day the phone rang. It was a man in the village whom we hardly knew. When I heard his name, I kept wondering why he was calling us. He told me about an incident that had happened the day before. Apparently some kids had taken toothpaste and written graffiti all over Arthur's car. (Funny, I opened a new toothpaste package this morning.) He asked if we knew who had done it. I said "No." He asked if we could ask our children if they knew anything about it. I said that I would ask, but was sure they didn't know anything. When I asked John he said he hadn't a clue. It was just as I suspected.

The next day we received another phone call from the village: another incident with the toothpaste transgressor. Again the request: "Can you please talk to your children?" Again, I agreed without giving it too much thought. That night at the dinner table, I mentioned the phone call and the auto-toothpaste situation, and glanced over at the children; I couldn't believe my eyes. There was my little Sara looking as guilty as I have ever seen her. The truth came out little by little. She and her friend Nicole had drawn a line from front to back on both sides of Arthur's car. Not once, but twice! I was shocked, appalled, and embarrassed.

There was nothing left to do but swallow our pride, go to Arthur, and apologize. I was mortified, but I knew we had to do it. My husband Ronnie told Sara and Nicole that they had to come with us, confess, apologize, and make amends. The girls didn't want to ask for Arthur's forgiveness, but they didn't have a choice. Arthur and Lynn were really great about the whole situation. Sara agreed to not only clean the car, but to help Lynn clean their entire house.

The next day as I walked back to my home, I stopped at Arthur's to share the mushrooms I had just picked. They were so understanding and forgiving that my guilt worsened. I felt the need to confess that Ronnie and I were really the ones responsible for the toothpaste. When Arthur looked confused, I admitted that we had talked badly about our neighbors, which had created the problem in the first place. As we expressed our desire to have a warm and friendly relationship with them, we hugged, made amends, forgave, and vowed to wipe the slate clean and start over.

When I returned home, I told Sara what had happened and her comment was, "So we are not going to make fun of Arthur and Lynn any more?" It hit me right in the face; the attitudes we imprint in our children's heads by saying things about people behind their backs are taken seriously and our words are put into action.

I learned who the awful neighbors were and it wasn't whom I'd originally judged.

**_Astrid Stahlberg_**

When you travel, you are often warned of people who may try to take advantage of you. People will tell you horror stories about people stealing, begging, harassing you and making your journey less than pleasant. It is rare that someone will share a story about one who doesn't want to take advantage but rather wants to contribute to the enjoyment of their experience. Linda Coverdale shares a refreshing tale of human connection that also serves as a lovely mirror of her.

# Trust

Jamaica

≫ ≪

*We make a living by what we get, we make a life by what we give.*

### *Sir Winston Churchill*

It was my first trip to Jamaica. I was fascinated by absolutely everything. There were so many new sights, smells, sounds, people, and customs, I couldn't wait to explore this new corner of the earth. The first morning, my roommate Leslie and I went across the road to a beautiful beach for an early morning swim. The sun was just up, the beach was clean, and there were very few people, so it was truly perfect. We laid down our cover-ups and shoes as we loped off toward the water. Just then, a little barefoot boy around seven years old approached us. He stopped us with his question.

"Do you want to buy some?" he asked. He had several strands of beads hanging around his neck.

"Not today, thanks," we said as we started toward the surf. He followed us with his arm outstretched with the necklaces reaching out for us. I looked over my shoulder and shrugged. "Besides we have no money with us." I gestured to my bathing suit.

"Don't you have someone at home to bring a present to?" he asked me as he walked down to the surf with us.

With his question, I immediately thought of my three young nieces who would be delighted that I remembered them. I could see their eyes light up with this gift from a far-off land. But I said instead, "I don't think so. What's your name?"

"Simon," he said.

"Well, Simon, if you are around later when we finish our meeting, maybe then . . . we'll see."

He reached over and put a strand around my neck. "There," he exclaimed. "They look pretty on you."

I took off the beads and handed them back to him saying, "No, Simon. I can't take them."

Immediately, he put the necklaces back around my neck. "You can wear them for breakfast, see how they feel. If you like them, you can pay me later."

"Simon, I can't do that. I may never see you again. How do you know I won't run off with the beads and never pay you."

"You won't. You are a good lady. I trust you."

Well, I hardly knew what to say. Never in my life had any salesperson ever entrusted me with anything. Never had a stranger trusted me with merchandise they were selling. Never had someone been so open and trusting of me.

Leslie and I went back to the hotel and prepared for breakfast. At breakfast our guide explained the economic conditions in Jamaica. She explained that many people lived in extreme poverty. She told us that for many this was their only way to make a living. She encouraged us to buy something, anything at all from the local merchants. If we didn't want anything we should just smile and say, "No thank you." But she encouraged us to treat every person we met with respect. She glanced over at me and noticed that I had a string of beads around my neck.

"It looks as if someone has been shopping already," she said.

"Well, sort of, but I haven't paid for it yet." I explained and told the story of Simon, and how he trusted me to keep the beads till after breakfast. She was aghast! She shook her head.

"That just doesn't happen! I can't believe it" she exclaimed.

As we came out from breakfast, Simon was standing there. I went to him and bought three strands of beads from him, as did Leslie.

We were busy with our travel agent duties, inspecting hotels. I didn't see Simon around. A couple of days later, when we were gathering on a bus to travel to the next destination, Simon came running up to me. Putting my arm around his shoulder, I asked, "So, Simon, what did you do with all that money you earned the other day?"

"I gave it to my mom. She bought shoes with the money."

"That's good. But now you probably want me to buy some more beads," I joked.

"No," Simon said, extending his hand to shake mine. "No ma'am, I just came to say thank you."

*Linda Coverdale*

War has a way of dividing people. There are those who are for it and those who are against it. There are those who are on "our side" and those who are on "the other side." By its very nature, war is divisive. Every once in a while, a person sees that we are all one . . . which makes the difference. Lee Hill-Nelson shares her firsthand experience of seeing the "mirror" of war.

## An About-Face

United States

⋙ ⋘

*The best way to destroy an enemy is to make him a friend.*

**Abraham Lincoln**

Dusk had settled in when the phone rang. It was my friend Joe, who was in sick bay, recuperating from the flu.

"Hey, Tex! Bring me and my buddy a malted milk from Ship's Store," he said. "Chow was no good tonight."

I told him I'd be right over.

I quickly dressed in my WAVE uniform. It was wartime, and we in the voluntary women's branch of the U.S. Navy always dressed in full uniform when we left the barracks. I looked in the mirror and straightened my shoulders, reminding myself that I served in the greatest navy in the world. Outside, the Wasatch Mountains outlined the sky. As I looked across the peaceful Utah valley, it was hard to believe there was a war raging in other lands.

Ship's Store made good malted milks, thick, with lots of ice cream, malt, and whole milk beaten until foamy, all for twenty-five cents. I got two and headed for sick bay.

"This is my buddy, Franz," said Joe as he motioned to the bed next to him.

My gaze wandered briefly around sick bay and observed that it was almost empty. The few patients who were there wore navy hospital pajamas and looked alike.

"We're sure hungry for those malts," Franz said. I turned my head back sharply at the sound of Franz's heavy German accent and stared at his face. He was German, a prisoner of war. The enemy. Why had Joe asked me to bring a malt to a Nazi?

I didn't even want to give him the malted milk, but because Joe had asked me to, I handed it to Franz. He smiled, and I forced a smile back.

The year was 1945, and as the war in Europe wound down, prisoners of war were brought to the Naval Supply Depot here at Clearfield, Utah. Tight security prevailed around the prisoners. Shore Patrols wearing guns and holsters guarded them. Posted rules stated that only authorized personnel were to talk with the prisoners, but no rules kept the rest of us from seeing and observing them.

We watched them every day, as if they were in a regimental review, in early mornings and late afternoons as they marched the famous goose-step to and from work, with perfect straight lines, eyes straight ahead.

They were precise and well trained, and the only indication that they might have any feelings at all came when they whistled tunes like "Beer Barrel Polka" and "Lili Marlene," or when one spat on the ground, showing, we thought, his attitude toward us Americans. Some prisoners were young boys, under eighteen; others were men in their late thirties or early forties. We assumed most of the in-betweens had met their death in the war.

At Clearfield, prisoners cared for the grounds, making the grass and flowers bloom like never before. Hard work seemed to fit them.

So it seemed strange, with all the rules on the base, that in the hospital Joe and one of those prisoners of war could be friends. Why, I wondered again, had Joe asked me to bring a malted milk to an enemy?

Bewildered, I sat down and listened as the two boys continued talking, Joe with his thick Chicago brogue and Franz in heavily accented English. They spoke easily and good-naturedly, discussing their homes and families, their governments, and the war. I marveled at Joe's willingness to accept Franz as a friend, and his treatment of Franz gradually eased my defenses. I studied Franz carefully.

Noting his blond hair and sad blue eyes, I could see he was young, probably about the age of my youngest brother. *The same age as my youngest brother!* The comparison hit me like a slap in the face. My little brother was still at home in high school, and this boy in front of me had just come out of combat as a prisoner of war!

"I'm glad to be in Clearfield," Franz was saying. "Some of my friends had to go to Idaho to pick beets. I hope President Truman will let us go home soon."

Why, this young German boy lying in bed was a real person, as real as Joe or my little brother! He wanted to be at home with his family just as much as we all did. What's more, he probably had been pressed into service, fighting in a war he hadn't asked for.

That evening, in sick bay, the harsh rules of war melted over a couple of milkshakes. Instead of fighting, enemies lay side by side, sharing their lives and becoming friends. Over the next few days, while Joe and Franz remained in sick bay, I spent my evenings visiting two friends instead of one. Joe, Franz, and I laughed together, swapped jokes, and shared stories about our families and homes in Texas, Chicago, and Germany. Our friendship made the world seem smaller, less complicated, and it filled me with hope for a peace that went beyond treaties and cease-fires.

When Franz left sick bay, he went back to the prisoner of war group, and sometimes I would catch a glimpse of him marching by, serious again, looking neither to the right nor left, seeing no one. But I saw him—and his fellow prisoners—with a different eye than I had before.

Soon after, Joe was discharged and went home to Chicago, and I was transferred to San Francisco for three months before going home to Texas. And I like to think that when Franz returned to Germany, he remembered the sailor who, without hesitation, treated him with brotherly love and the WAVE who, though it took a while, did an about-face.

*Lee Hill-Nelson*

The world can seem a safe place until political situations change. What was safe one day can become threatening the next. There are some people, however, who cling to their benevolence regardless of the current political conditions. Fear can paralyze, but genuine kindness opens all doors. Charles Kastner learned about the mirrors of compassion.

# Trust Thy Neighbor

Seychelles

⋙ ⋘

*Every great man is always being helped by everybody, for his gift is to get good out of all things and all persons.*

### John Ruskin

My wife and I hadn't planned on spending Thanksgiving Day huddled in our little house in the jungle-covered mountains, sticky and damp from the equatorial heat. We had planned to attend the dinner being held by the American chargé d'affaires, a dinner that held the promise of real turkey and pumpkin pie. We were more than slightly concerned for our safety since we had been forced to turn back by a police officer who told us there was "trouble in town."

Waves of heat radiated off the pavement in front of our house, distorting the shapes of the soldiers who patrolled our road. They were looking for the mercenaries who had come to our island and destroyed everything we had taken for granted. The group of mercenaries had been discovered on an incoming flight, and had planned to overthrow the government of Mahe, the island upon which we lived. They took over the control tower and the leader managed to hijack a plane from India. In order to cover his escape he left a cadre of men behind to hold off the Seychelles security forces. This group then "melted" into the surrounding hills.

When we returned to our little house, we switched on Radio Seychelles and heard the news that security forces were scouring the island for the remaining mercenaries, one of whom happened—to my horror—to match my description exactly. I had visions of burly policemen hauling me off for interrogation, followed by an execution; or an equally unpleasant prospect of local vigilantes murdering us right in our beds. Our little island suddenly seemed more mousetrap than paradise, with us being the mice cornered in our tiny house.

We stayed inside, huddled together as we listened to the radio's constant plea for all citizens to keep a watchful eye out for all foreigners. These announcements seemed to make my wife physically ill, for she felt nauseous and light-headed. By the start of the second day under curfew, Mary and I were down to a few tea bags and a handful of rice. We feared that if we went to the local market we might be attacked.

Just then our neighbor, an old farmer, passed the house. Mary and I had often seen the man and his wife walking up the little path right before sunset, with huge bundles of grass balanced on their heads. They seemed happy yet very poor, shoeless and in tattered clothing. Mary called softly to the man and he came to our back door, which was hidden from the road. He told us he was ignoring the curfew because he needed to find feed for his animals. After some small talk and an awkward pause, Mary asked him if he would buy us some food.

His expression turned serious as Mary pushed a twenty rupee note at him. He pushed the money back at her and said, "Plenty of trouble still in town. You better stay inside." Then he turned and left, ignoring our calls to come back as he hurried down the path to the road, disappearing around a corner. We felt even more isolated and alone than before our conversation. We spent the rest of the day hiding in the house, with Mary in the bathroom agonizing over her stomachache.

Later that day, Mary whispered to me, "Chuck, someone is knocking on the back door." I jumped up, feeling certain that our moment of truth had arrived; the security forces had finally come to haul us away. I somehow found the courage to crack open the door as my heart pounded. I didn't see any snarling militiamen with AK-47 rifles, only the old farmer's tranquil face. Relaxed and relieved, I wondered why he had returned. Maybe he had decided to give us a second chance if we made it "worth his while."

I saw he had a sack in his hand. He smiled at us and pulled out a bag of rice, another bag of lentils, and a can of condensed milk. He pushed them into my arms and started walking away. "Wait," I fumbled for words, "please take some money." "No, no. Good day," he said, waving to us as he climbed the path.

Mary and I couldn't move, stunned by the old man's kindness. Tears ran down our cheeks. We were amazed and relieved to realize that we didn't have to be afraid of everyone. We knew there was at least one person, and possibly many more, who would help us if we asked them. His gesture showed us the main thing we lost in the coup was our trust in the kindness of our neighbors.

After a few days, the security forces caught the mercenaries, and life slowly returned to normal. We survived the coup with a new faith in the basic kindness of humans. My wife's stomach pains turned out to be the first sign of a temporary medical condition that ended with the birth of our beautiful daughter!

*Charles Kastner*

Mirrors come in many packages. When two people say the same words at the same time, say something that someone else is thinking; or when two of you unknowingly wear the same colors; these are all moments that confirm an undeniable, unconscious connection. You know at that moment that you are connected and mirroring the same internal reality. Francesco Garripoli shares with us his mirror that is beyond words.

# Beyond Words

## China

*A real friend is one who walks in when the rest of the world walks out.*

**Walter Winchell**

I didn't realize Beijing would be so cold in November. The ubiquitous smell of sulfur coal travels on freezing gusts that snake their way through the cracks in my tiny room. This concrete cubicle dormitory, without carpet, heat, or water, is still a gift from the Universe for which I am grateful. Illuminated by the same buzzing fluorescent light fixture that everyone here in the city uses, I am reminded of my connection to each person in this city . . . a city that embraces me.

Though twice as old as most people here, I am a student once again, as if the learning in life *ever* stops. *"Yuan fen,"* the Mandarin name for destiny, has brought me together with twenty-five Chinese students. They range in age from fourteen to twenty-one. They have come from all over their country to learn the ancient healing art of *Qigong* (pronounced "chee gung."). This is our common bond, and I too am here to learn. Qigong may be our only link since we don't share our culture, belong to the same generation, or communicate with a common language.

Yet each time my eyes connected with one of my fellow students, I was continually reminded that those differences were, in fact, an illusion.

With one student I felt an instant affinity. I fell into her catlike gaze, lasting only for brief moments at a time, then quickly swept away by the cultural rules that govern contact with strangers. We'd laugh at the simultaneous awareness that we shared something special in our fleeting encounters. We'd look at a flower together and nod in agreement. We knew we were on the same wavelength. Since Qigong is a lifestyle, a health practice that works with energy, we were accustomed to exploring realms beyond the intellectual. Even so, the motivation to communicate with words, a human aspiration, can limit possibilities because of basic assumptions.

Our passion to be alive overflowed our emotional reservoirs and flooded our minds, driving us to share what we felt. My new friend and I were at that precipice, yet without a common language to build a bridge between our separate realities.

I went to my dorm and began teaching myself Chinese characters, one at a time. If I could at least copy the ones I needed, I would be able to write my friend a note. This daunting task brought me face-to-face with even more challenges as the Chinese grammar and language structure are completely different from my Romance language roots. There are no plurals, no genders, no sense of past-present-future. On top of that, each character is a concept or a story much more than just a mere word. How am I to write even a short note, facing the daunting task of mastering this chasm between us?

The gift of the written word is something I have often taken for granted. It's that miraculous link between the inner and the outer worlds. I sat in my room, pen in hand, and I was blocked. I've always loved to write, watching the words flow like nectar, surprising myself as they appear on the page, emerging from my pen like gossamer from a spider. At that moment, I was trapped in a web spun from my feelings of separation and my intense desire to connect.

However, I'm not one to give up easily. I trust that intention carries us beyond form . . . in this case, beyond the Chinese characters that I might select. It was an opportunity to release my need to be eloquent. It was my chance to forget about coming across as intelligent or worldly. I had a feeling in my heart that I wanted to convey and, if what I purported to believe was true, then my desire would ride on my intention like clouds on the wind.

I set out to draw four characters, "wo," "gaoxing," "ni," and "pengyou." This translates to "I happy you friend." After my aspirations to write my essay, and my inner wrestling with the characters I would choose, I found that in the simplest form those sentiments were what I wanted to say after all. I drew these characters over a small painting I did of a bamboo branch with a mountain in the background to symbolize growth and stability.

That evening at 11:00 P.M., just like every other night for the past month, we met in the Institute's courtyard. With studies and duties behind us, these few moments in the shadows were our time to laugh and share the experiences of the day, all without words, except for tonight. I revealed the note I had so carefully worked on that afternoon and handed it to my young friend. She took it, covering her mouth to muffle her laughter. As it was too dark to read, she simply put it in her pocket, said good night, and turned to walk away. Within two steps, she turned back toward me and with an extended hand, offered me a piece of paper. I accepted it and she ran into the darkened dormitory.

Smiling, I held my gift and returned to my room, warm with joy and anticipation. I dared not turn on the mood-altering fluorescent light, so I walked over to the single window to read this little note by the moon-light. Unfolding the delicate paper that was folded origami-style into a swan, I made out four roughly-hewn English words. They read, "I happy you friend."

I covered the note to guard it from the moisture in my eyes.

*Francesco Garripoli*

# RULE 8 EIGHT

## WHAT YOU MAKE OF YOUR LIFE IS UP TO YOU

*You have all the tools and resources you need.*
*What you do with them is up to you.*

It is easier to understand the concept that what you make of your life is up to you when you think of people who are privileged. It is not always easy to see the application when a child is raised in poverty with very few resources. It appears as if this child has limited exposure, options, and opportunities. When a door opens and someone sees a spark of connection with his/her purpose in life, this is a truly magical moment. Maria Tereza Maldonado shares the spark of connection.

# Seeds of Solidarity

Brazil

⇒ ⇐

*No great man lives in vain.*
*The history of the world is but the biography of great men.*

### *Benjamin Disraeli*

Mark, a fifteen-year-old boy, lives in one of the seven hundred slums in Rio de Janeiro. In the narrow, dirty, medieval-like streets, there are hundreds of small houses built out of brick and wood in a precarious balance. Up there, in those tiny houses, thousands of people live and work hard to earn so little that it is barely enough money to buy food and clothes for their families. Many unemployed men spend the day drinking while their wives work and older children care for the younger ones. It is a powerful contrast seeing the extreme poverty of the slums, with a wonderful view of white sand beaches, the deep blue sea, and other mountains.

Some of Mark's friends are school dropouts who hang around the streets stealing, smoking pot, drinking, and fighting with kids from other gangs. Two of his best friends had a run-in with the police and were killed in the "drug war." Many times Mark felt the temptation to join them, but he always remembered his father's advice: "Living in peace with a little money is better than living in fear with a lot of money." But Mark thought, "I don't want to become a taxi driver like my father; I want more in life, I just don't know what."

For the drug dealers, the narrow and irregular streets where no cars can pass offer safe hiding places for their illegal business. On the top of the mountains, they build real fortresses full of modern and powerful guns to guarantee that no one, not even the police, would interfere with the drug traffic. The temptation to make more money in one week than their parents earn in a month seduces many teenagers to get involved with drug dealers. High-risk business for young people living in such precarious conditions make it difficult to have dreams for a better future.

One day, the news circulated that a computer science school would start the next month so that children between ages six and seventeen could learn how to use a computer. The project was coordinated by a young man who had been doing volunteer work since he was twelve years old. He had a dream of teaching computer science to people in low-income communities in order to create new opportunities for life dreams. Initially, he was severely criticized. People said, "These people want money to buy food, not computers!" The shock was that on the very first day four hundred people registered for the course. One of the registrations was Mark's.

As soon as Mark started to learn how to write text using a computer, he had his first lesson on how to navigate through the Internet. Mark was fascinated by the opportunities that were opening up before his eyes. He thought, "Now I know what I want my life to be about. I want to teach computer science to other kids, and to my friends involved with drug dealers; I want to help them open other options in their lives!"

In one year, Mark was recognized as one of the best students of the school. He received a scholarship in Web design, and volunteered to become a teacher. The project grew quickly. In a few years, more than a hundred computer schools were opened in other slums in Rio de Janeiro. Later, the course spread to other cities and then to other countries. Thousands of teenagers now have an opportunity to build a meaningful life. Most of them volunteer, teaching other kids what they've learned and spreading the seeds of solidarity wherever there is good soil to allow them to grow.

*Maria Tereza Maldonado*

Seeing opportunities before they have revealed themselves and allowing them to happen is a talent. When a spark is ignited in one person's head or heart and it starts a chain reaction that benefits everyone, it shows synergy. Greenhouses not only grow lettuce, sometimes they grow people. Christine Wotowiec shows us how the domino effect can positively affect many lives.

## Lettuce in Cairo

Egypt

⇒ ⇐

*You must first have a lot of patience to learn to have patience.*

### *Stanislaw J. Lec*

The picture in the brochure showed a young boy sleeping inside a large truck tire. Thin and dirty, dressed in rags, he was a street boy in Cairo, Egypt.

"There are thousands of boys like this in Cairo," the woman at the orphanage told us. "Their bed can be under a bridge, on a sidewalk, or huddled next to a donkey down an alleyway. It's a heart-wrenching fact of life."

Large, overpopulated cities around the world struggle with the plight of the homeless, and Cairo is no exception. At the same time, it is a city of splendid historic wonders, with some of the friendliest people any-where. Tourism is one of its major industries. Tourists are always warned not to drink the water or eat uncooked vegetables, especially lettuce. Little is said about the street boys.

My husband Pete and I had come to the Cairo orphanage with a plan to benefit both the street boys and the tourists. Many of the youngsters taken in by the orphanage stay there through adolescence. As they approach adulthood, they need to learn skills that will serve them for the rest of their lives. The orphanage directors had been seeking a small business for the boys to run, something they could handle themselves. That's where we came in.

"Lettuce—are you crazy?" they asked us. Most of Cairo's locally grown lettuce is irrigated and washed by canal water. The canal water is not safe for drinking. It can also harbor a parasite that gets into the soil and then into the leafy vegetables. When ingested, the parasite can cause liver damage and even death.

What we had in mind, though, was a hydroponic lettuce greenhouse. "Hydroponic vegetables are grown without soil, in a nutrient-rich water solution that is filtered and virtually free of contaminants," Pete explained to the doubters. "They're grown in a controlled greenhouse, which can extend the growing season and create nearly picture-perfect lettuce. They'll be safe for anyone to eat!"

The orphanage staff realized that tourists and Egyptians alike would welcome having fresh, safe greens to eat. Young Ali, a former social worker at the orphanage, was quickly appointed manager of the proposed green-house. He soon pulled together a "staff" of older boys from the orphanage.

Pete and I had only a three-month visa, so we had to work fast. The greenhouse had to be built; the boys had to be trained; markets had to be researched. There were many challenges along the way, everything from the language barrier to a lack of building supplies.

But with each day of training and progress, the bond grew among the team members. We ate together, laughed together, and worked very hard together. We became friends. I nicknamed one youngster "Smiley," for the constant smile he wore despite the harshness and pain he had already experienced in life. He in turn named me "Mrs. Flower"—how apt for a horticulturist!

From groundbreaking to the first sown seed, we shared it all. Soon, the seeds became seedlings, and our lettuce matured rapidly. Our public open house was just days away. Cairo was about to see the hard work and accomplishments of these former street boys. In turn, we hoped a whole new world of opportunities would open for them.

But then came disaster. For three days, a huge sandstorm swept over the region, battering our greenhouse. We couldn't venture outside our hotel. We could only wait it out, and worry.

When the storm subsided, Pete and I walked to the torn, bent, and battered greenhouse. The sea of green lettuce was covered in dust and sand.

"How can this be happening?" I whispered to Pete, as tears streamed down my cheeks. "Everything we all worked for, all those opportunities . . . destroyed!"

He could only stand there, speechless.

Suddenly, the silence was broken.

"Good morning, Mrs. Flower," announced Smiley. He stood there with a broom in his hand, backed by the rest of the team, laden with tools, brooms, and buckets.

With lumps in our throats, we stared at our undaunted crew. As I looked at these onetime street boys, I realized that if they could handle this challenge, they were more than ready to run this business on their own. This was the ultimate test.

Ali gave us a thumbs-up signal and a gentle smile, and then we began. We worked, cleaned, and rebuilt. We gently rinsed the dust-choked lettuce with pure water. On the day of our open house, the greenhouse stood a bit crooked after its battering. But inside, all was clean and green and ready for business. Cairo was impressed.

A year later, Pete and I returned to the orphanage. There was the same greenhouse, still battered and sandblasted. There were our same dear friends, eager to greet us. There were even the same discussions about building supplies and construction permits. Only this time we weren't having those discussions—the boys were. Those onetime street boys had had so much success selling lettuce in Cairo they were building another greenhouse to keep up with the demand!

*Christine Wotowiec*

When life deals us a hand that we didn't choose, we don't always see that what we make of it is up to us. Some people will give up. Others will complain. Gabrielle Haubner shares how she took charge and turned her experience of being a victim into becoming victorious.

## It's Never Too Late

Austria/ United Kingdom

≫ ≪

*Change before you have to.*

### *Jack Welch*

Having grown up in the most loving, financially secure environment, I expected my life to go down this same wonderful road, full of love, success, and contentment. So, when I fell in love and a couple of months later became pregnant, I decided to marry the father. Once our boy was out of the pram we had a baby girl. Their father turned out to be anything but a family man and before being dragged down with him I divorced him, finished my studies, and started a life of my own. Starting a career in teaching seemed the right thing to do as it gave me the option to spend weekends and holidays with my children. My parents were again a huge support and my mother helped with the kids. I was on my way to a better life.

Then it happened again. I fell in love. He was seven years younger, which at the age of twenty-seven is a big difference. He seemed to be very mature for his age and when he proposed I took the risk. Knowing that a marriage certificate is not a warranty for life, I tried my best to make it work. I supported him all the way when he wanted to go to college, even though I found it increasingly difficult to stretch one salary to pay for the mortgage, two children, and all the other bills. I did not complain, however, since I encouraged him to pursue this career path.

The summer before his final year in college we went on a holiday in Greece. That's where it happened. He befriended a sweet, young, blond German girl and her friend. He did not return to our room before 3 or 4 A.M. night after night and even during the day he spent more time with them than with us, his family. I did not wish to ruin my holiday any more by making a big scene, so I concentrated on having a good time with the kids.

Once back home, it turned out that he had been exchanging love letters with the blond, complaining about the children and me. That was the beginning of the end. Another marriage down the drain.

Two years and a few boyfriends later I was suicidal, feeling completely unable to keep a relationship going. It didn't take long until I ended up in the hospital. With the help of therapists and the love of my entire family I began to recover.

There I was: thirty-five years old, divorced for the second time, two children from the first marriage, stuck in a job I did not like anymore, in a town that I hated. I was in a rut and I was depressed. Very depressed.

And then I decided to take charge of my life. I realized that I had to get some distance from the protective love of my parents, from the job that confronted me with the terrible misery of some of my students and the town I so hated. After having been on holiday in London with my two children, I asked them how they felt about moving to England. They were twelve and fourteen, before boyfriends or girlfriends became so important, and they were on board.

I started preparing. I felt good. Six months later we left Austria on three one-way tickets to London. It was a dramatic step, with dramatic good-byes, and seeing my Mum cry almost broke my heart, but I knew I had to go. I needed proof that I could lead a successful, happy life. I rented a little terraced house in the southeast of London, since I had to wait for my apartment in Austria to be sold before I could afford to buy my own place. Six months later we moved into a wonderful three-bedroom house with a garden and lovely neighbors. Still trying out various jobs, from teaching to waiting tables, I was happy. The kids loved their new home, they were doing well at school and even my son, who hated learning in Austria, decided he wanted to stay in school longer than he had planned.

It has now been almost eight years since I have left my hometown. I have finally settled in a middle-management job with a big American airline, based in London, that has recognized and rewarded my common sense and business acumen and I am making enough money for a comfortable living.

My son has developed a huge interest in computers and the Internet and has managed to turn his hobby into a satisfying and well-paid job.

He has his own little flat with a cat to keep him company. We get along very well and I am proud of both of us, seeing what a fine young man he has become.

My daughter has left the nest to go to university, studying theatre-TV and drama and she is doing very well at her courses.

I concentrate on my career, happy not having to worry about how to get and keep a boyfriend. I did it. I made it in a foreign country with no help from family or friends. Just on my own. I have not looked back ever since and I definitely have not regretted a single day. I still go to see my parents and the rest of my family, but at the end of the day I look forward to going home.

Sometimes, I feel like I need a change again, and when the time comes, I will pack my suitcases and start all over again somewhere else. I did it once and I know now I can do it again. If I could take an unhappy, depressed, and stuck life as a single mother trying to make ends meet, and turn it around, I believe anyone can who is willing to make a change.

*Gabrielle Haubner*

We can either believe that our actions don't make a difference or we can believe that whatever we do matters. Miraculous things happen when you believe in possibilities. Anne Colledge shares with us her fruity story that forever changed her beliefs.

# My First Apple Tree

United Kingdom

⋙ ⋘

*Everyone has his day and some days last longer than others.*

### *Sir Winston Churchill*

"If your apple tree doesn't get an apple on it this summer, it'll have to be chopped down. It's a waste of space," said my mother. She was the practical one. She had to be. It was 1942, wartime in England. There was rationing and little food to spare, and little money to buy it with. When Uncle Bill had first given me the little apple tree to start, Mum said, "No."

"It'll be too big for our garden and will take the goodness from the vegetables. We need those vegetables," she said.

"We'll put it at the end of the garden," my dad coaxed. "It'll do no harm there."

So the cutting was put in, but to my disappointment, year after year it had no blossoms.

"Waste of space," my mother said each year. And today, she gave her ultimatum. An apple this summer, or no apple tree at all.

I shivered. Dad caught my eye and winked, but the loving little signal just brought tears to my eyes. I ran out of the house and up the road to my Aunt Liz's house. I flung open her garden gate and saw her huge apple tree. The sun shone on each shiny red and green apple hanging on the heavy branches. I stared at it for so long that I could still see it when I closed my eyes. I wanted a tree like that in my garden more than anything in the whole world.

As I stared into the branches, I started to see pictures, first of the apple tree in winter, its strong black skeleton of branches white with snow and frost. Then, in the spring, covered in white blossoms, giving way to tiny buds that swelled up into huge apples, knobby and misshapen.

In the summer, the children played under the shade of the tree. At harvest time, Uncle Bill climbed carefully up the wooden ladder leaning against the tree. He passed the apples to us to put in wicker clothes baskets, gently, so as not to bruise them.

We children ran up and down the street knocking on each door giving everyone a bag full of apples.

"Aunt Liz sends these," we said at every house. There were apples for everyone.

We ate apples for weeks—apple pie, applesauce, apple jam. My favorite was baked apples, smothered in thick yellow custard lying deep in the bowls. Apples we couldn't eat right away were stored under the bed during winter. They gave off a sweet, musty smell. They lasted for months until their skins wrinkled or became bruised and we children pushed our fingers into the brown mush, and got in trouble for it.

I loved everything about the apple tree and that was why I wanted a tree myself so badly.

"It's getting late, honey," Aunt Liz said, walking up to the tree. "You'd better go home now, or your mum will wonder where you are."

When I got back from Aunt Liz's, I went to look at my tree. As I stared into the branches, I willed it with all my heart to burst into bud, to flower into apples, just like Aunt Liz's tree. And suddenly, there it was amid the branches. An apple. An apple!

I ran into the house, shrieking in excitement. "Mum, Mum, there's an apple on my tree!"

My mother and father ran out into the garden.

"Well, I never," Mum said in amazement.

My father started to laugh. My mother went up to the tree.

"Fred," she accused, "It's tied on with string." She glared at him, and he grinned at her. And then he winked at me.

Mum shook her head at her two impractical apple tree lovers. She sighed in exasperation. But she never suggested cutting the tree down after that.

Now, years later, my apple tree bears fruit every autumn. It fed us during the lean war years and still feeds us now when food is easier to come by. That's what apple trees are for, for food and memories that no one can take away. They take a long time to grow, but, like all good things, the wait is worth it.

*Anne Colledge*

L ife has a funny way of supporting our intentions. We must be careful what we wish for because we may just get it. Errol Broome shares with us a clear demonstration of the power of thought.

# Tea Time

Australia

➤ ❦

*To generous souls every task is noble.*

**Euripides**

On a wildly windy day, I was running late for my appointment at Jean's house. I grabbed a handful of lemon balm from my garden, in case she was feeling as frazzled as I was.

I intended to stop along the way and pick a sprig of eucalyptus leaves. They make a reviving cup of tea when mixed with lemon balm. Eucalyptus grow nearly everywhere in our Australian town. I was sure I could find one on the way to Jean's.

Each street I passed was lined with elm, ash, or plane trees. There were plenty of melaleucas and an occasional grevillea, but I couldn't find just the right eucalyptus tree. Here and there a majestic giant towered above roofs, but I'm not the sort to scale death-defying heights for a cup of tea.

So I arrived without the eucalyptus leaves.

"What do I do with these?" asked Jean, when I handed her the lemon balm.

"Not much," I said, ashamed of my meager offering. "You really need eucalyptus leaves to make a good cup of tea."

Jean took me into her back garden. There was a eucalyptus tree near the back fence. But it was a whopper—its lowest leaves were far beyond our reach. We turned inside and made a cup of coffee.

The next day, the wind was still blowing hard. And the lemon balm leaves still sat in a glass on Jean's windowsill.

"What do you plan to do with these?" her husband Ted asked.

Jean repeated my recipe. "They make a good cup of tea, but we need fresh eucalyptus leaves," she said.

Just then, an ear-splitting crash thundered around them. The house shuddered. Jean and Ted raced out the back door—and found the huge eucalyptus tree lying at their feet.

Jean has always been a believer in the power of positive thinking.

She made a nice pot of lemon balm-eucalyptus tea before she called to have the tree removed.

"Next time you want some tea," Ted said, pondering the $500 bill for tree removal, "Just ask for a cup, but be careful what you ask for!"

*Errol Broome*

It is easier to be a Negaholic and say that unusual and out of the ordinary things cannot happen. After all, if they are not logical and reasonable, they may seem crazy. This unreasonable story really happened.

## No Limits

Lithuania

➤ ⋲

*There is an enormous amount of goodness and goodwill*
*and right feeling and action in the modern world.*

### *Sir Richard Livingstone*

In the darkest days of World War II, when Lithuania was invaded by the Red Army, and then overrun by the Nazis, Valdus Adamkus was a teenage boy. When Lithuania was occupied in 1941, he became an active member of the underground movement. Because he was supporting the resistance, the Gestapo was in pursuit of him; he was wanted for his anti-Soviet activities, but he kept one step ahead of Stalin's secret police. When the Soviets chased the Germans out of the Baltic States, Adamkus and his family knew it was time to flee Lithuania. He had to grow up quickly, and leaving his roots made him fear that he might never see his homeland free.

Adamkus settled in Chicago, home to America's largest Lithuanian American community. His early days were difficult, "I began from almost nothing, working in a factory, working at night and learning English during the day." His first priority was to obtain an education. Through his diligence and determination, he became a powerful man in his adopted country, but despite his success he never stopped thinking about his imprisoned homeland.

Adamkus felt a deep moral obligation to stay active in Lithuanian American groups; he wanted to do everything possible to free his countrymen left behind and give them the opportunity to experience the independence he had. But it seemed as though only a miracle could bring about the fall of communism.

That miracle occurred in 1991 when the Soviet Union collapsed. Lithuania seized its independence, but not without a struggle. His people were impoverished, starving, and beset with problems, but they were free.

When his country became independent, Adamkus applied for and received Lithuanian citizenship. He became a familiar figure in Lithuania, and his contacts there offered him an entry into politics. But when it was first announced that he would run for the presidency of Lithuania even his own advisors were somewhat incredulous. For Adamkus, the decisions had been difficult. He had to decide whether to leave the success and security he had worked so hard for in America, and to move his family away from their friends and their home. But Adamkus decided he must use his experience to contribute to the country that had given him life.

The race was a close fight; the candidates arrayed against Adamkus were mostly former communist officials. They criticized him and called him a carpetbagger who knew little if anything about present-day Lithuania. But Adamkus was undeterred; he pressed forward, emphasizing how his experience could help Lithuania reach its full potential. In January, the final phase of the election was held. When the ballots were counted, Adamkus had won by eleven thousand votes.

When asked about the task he has just undertaken, Adamkus replied, "I realize it is not going to be easy . . . I am happy I have this opportunity because it proves only one thing: There are no limits in life." He was an exile from his homeland, an impoverished refugee, yet his love for his country and its people enabled him to become the man who would lead Lithuania into the future.

*Rob Reynolds*
*MSNBC*

# RULE 9 NINE

## ALL YOUR ANSWERS LIE INSIDE OF YOU

*All you need to do is look, listen, and trust.*

I nner guidance comes in many forms: illogical, irrational, and unreasonable directives, clear images, premonitions, dreams, repetitive images, words from friends, or strong and undeniable feelings. Whatever way your inner wisdom speaks to you, it will knock on your door until you finally listen to it or go numb in the process. You will never know why your intuition was beckoning to you unless you heed what it says. When you listen, pay attention, and do what it suggests, then it will be clear why it was trying to get your attention in the first place. Sibylle Alexander shows us an example of this.

# Listen to Inner Messages

Germany

➤ ❧

*Wisdom consists not so much in knowing what to do in the ultimate as knowing what to do next.*

### *Herbert Hoover*

Germany had its unsung heroes during the time of the Third Reich and George was one of them. He was a quiet old doctor who spoke very little and to whom people came from far and wide because he combined old wisdom with new knowledge and advised his patients how to heal themselves with herbs instead of drugs. He was a man that was able to heal the soul as well as the body.

Since the death of his wife he had developed a sixth sense with which to hear the silent cries for help. He slept lightly and would listen to any timid knock at his back door, which was left open both day and night. Life was dangerous for a man who helped Jews, Gypsies, priests, and pastors; George didn't differentiate between races or faiths.

When he did hear a knock in the middle of the night he would instantly run downstairs, open the door, and pull the person into his surgery room that had heavy blackout curtains. He did this before he even switched on the light or uttered a word. George knew that Gypsies had carved rune codes on his gate that identified him as a friend; he guessed that his address was passed on in synagogues abroad from person to person so that they would send word to those left behind. George never expected money from his "backdoor patients," yet he was pleased when a brown envelope arrived containing one thousand reichsmarks and a note with "Thank you" scrawled in haste.

In the small surgery, babies had been delivered whose mothers pleaded with him to hide the child after a brief naming ceremony. George found German women who were not afraid to foster a little Jewish child as long as a birth certificate could be forged. Often it meant long journeys in his battered car, procuring milk powder and diapers, building up a network of helpers sworn to secrecy. George lived with the expectation of a knock at his front door by men in uniform and therefore he destroyed all addresses after memorizing them. Strange prayers came from his lips for tiny Louise in Goethestrasse or baby Max at Sonnenhof.

As the war neared its end, George retired to the outskirts of Dresden. He tended his herb garden and acquired beehives. No Gypsies were left and hardly a Jew, but the habit of listening had stayed with George all these years. It had become an inner listening, so he was not surprised by a strange premonition he had. He was guided by an inner voice to pick large quantities of nettles, put them into barrels and fill them with rainwater.

George obeyed. Armed with thick gloves he went out to the hedgerows and rubbish dumps to collect nettles; he begged and borrowed every old barrel in the neighborhood and made nettle suds. A pungent smell invaded his garden as he waited. And then, not long after, one day the sirens wailed and bombs were falling from the sky; an inferno engulfed his city. People ran like living torches through the streets, children screamed in agony as their feet touched the melting asphalt. Invalids felt their beds begin to burn under them, and thousands perished.

Those who knew George fled to his house. He stripped them and plunged each man, woman, and child into one of his barrels. Oh what blissful relief! Never in his long life as a doctor had George experienced anything like this. The green baths had miraculous healing powers that did not diminish with the volume of patients who came to him. His garden looked like a medieval painting with heads sticking out of wooden barrels: a scene from the last judgment.

The nettle cure saved many lives. Years later, analysts discovered that this plant contains combudoron. Fifty years later we can buy Combudoron cream in any pharmacy to ease the scarring and pain of skin burns. George's inner guidance was unexplainable prior to Dresden on fire, however, to this day, he is grateful that he learned to listen to inner messages as well as outer sounds.

*Sibylle Alexander*

Inner messages come in many different forms. One of the forms they take is in doing seemingly impossible things for people who can't do anything for themselves. We are always in the right place at the right time to receive the messages that were intended for us. When you trust that, you know that you can't do anything wrong. Jan Burnes shows how her listening gave smiles to thousands of children.

# Teddy Bears

Romania/Australia

≫ ≪

*Kindness is more important than wisdom, and the recognition of this is the beginning of wisdom.*

**Theodore Isaac Rubin**

On a flight between London and Paris in the late '80s, I was reading my favorite magazine when I chanced upon an article on Romania. It described in vivid words and pictures the terrible plight of the babies in the Romanian orphanages.

My privileged surroundings blurred into tears of helpless rage as pictures of babies, two and three to a cot, sitting for days in their own urine and mess, floated up at me from the pages.

No love or care, no toys or relief from the stark boredom and night-mare that was "home" to thousands of babies abandoned by their poverty-stricken parents in a country where contraception was against the law and people were encouraged to have as many children as possible regardless of their ability to cope.

As I sat there, I realized that I could not live with my conscience if I didn't do something to help these little souls. A mother of two healthy, happy, much-loved and cosseted children, I realized at that moment that we all share a responsibility for little children, no matter what nationality or who their biological parents are.

I had my own business and was reasonably well off—jaunts to the south of France for some "time out" were a regular feature in my life. I decided, through the medium of my company, to do something to help these tragic orphans.

On my return to the office, and with the full support of my staff of twenty-five, I set up a public relations department, got in touch with the Romanian authorities in England, and gathered more information about the orphanages.

Many of them were already receiving aid from overseas, but the orphan-ages in the far northeastern section of the country had received nothing. They were too remote and the route was difficult and dangerous. Modern-day highwaymen lay in wait, robbing and killing indiscriminately.

I mailed out flyers to all my customers and my suppliers, to everyone in my local chamber of commerce and business network groups, and to local business people and schools. We organized Sunday fetes and garden parties and participated in business exhibitions. We appealed for teddy bears for Romanian orphans in every way our creative minds could think up!

Many of my staff volunteered to collect, wash, and repair the teddies for their journey. Some were actually the size of a small child, whilst others could be held in the palm of your hand. Little button eyes were fastened securely and wobbly limbs were reattached.

Within three weeks we had over three thousand teddy bears sitting in our factory—new and preloved, but all in excellent condition.

My one criteria for the teddy bears was that they looked as good as new. I didn't want any child to feel they were getting "shoddy goods."

I approached British Airways and they immediately offered to airfreight the teddies, free of charge, to Budapest, the capital of Romania. But then Romanian colleagues in England warned me that the cargo would probably be stolen off the tarmac at the airport; the teddies would be sold on the black market.

So I approached a local trucking company—would they provide two trucks and four drivers to make the journey across Europe to deliver the teddies to their tiny new owners? No small request!

The trucking company agreed instantly, the burly macho owner-manager almost reduced to tears when I explained the plight of the babies and toddlers.

Within a week the bears were packed and we were off on the long and dangerous trip across Europe. It took two weeks of almost nonstop driving to reach the orphanage, and we were all exhausted on our arrival. But when we started to hand out the teddies to the little children and saw their faces light up with joy, all the effort proved to be worthwhile.

Foreign aid workers had already arrived at the orphanage as a result of the publicity; the cots were clean and the children reasonably so. But the pride of ownership and the comfort they got from having their very own teddy bear was more important to these loveless children than clean linen.

When Jesus said, "Suffer the little children to come unto me," I believe it was a message to adults everywhere. We must be responsible for our future generation to ensure their emotional well-being. They need all the love and care possible to sustain them in their adult life.

*Jan Burnes*

In the industrialized world, we often fear death. We try to distance ourselves from the inevitability and reality of death until the very last moment. Elephants return to their birthplace to die and some people receive that message as well. In Meguido Zola's story, she shares an experience that demonstrates the fact that when you have truly lived, you are ready to embrace death. When your time comes, you know it, and you know where you must be.

# When the Time Is Right

Kenya

⇒ ⇐

*Never give up, for that is just the place and time that the tide will turn.*

**Harriet Beecher Stowe**

My teaching buddy, Norman, and I were taking a class of children to the rooftop of Africa—Mount Kilimanjaro. One afternoon, pausing after fording the final stream, I watched a lone figure emerge from the trailing fronds of liana. A frail, old woman balanced what looked like all her worldly possessions on her head. Catching sight of the children stretched out on the hillside, she let out a gasp of surprise.

"Ooooh! . . . So many children!" she gazed in wonder.

"Yes, Mama," I said. "Forty children."

"Forty?" her eyes widened. "God has truly blessed you."

"Yes . . ." I laughed. "Though, of course, they're not mine."

"But, see, you hold them in your hands."

"True, Mama. And I see God has blessed you, too—with many years."

"Twice forty years," she laughed. Then she volunteered where she had come from, a village several days away by foot. She then told where she was going, another village, several days' walking distance in the opposite direction.

I said, "You must be on an important safari," so as not to ask a direct question, which is considered intrusive.

"Yes . . . it is the safari of a lifetime. One only takes it once!" She explained she had left the place where she'd lived her entire adult life, married her husband, and raised her children and grandchildren. She said that she was returning to the village where, eighty years before, she'd been born. She said, "I am returning home to die, God willing."

"God willing, indeed, Mama," I said. "For the distance is great, the terrain is difficult, and you are full in years."

"True," the old woman laughed: "Though it won't be as difficult as you imagine, young man. You see, a long time ago, my heart got there first—long before my body. So now it will be easy enough for the rest of me to follow!"

**Meguido Zola**

There is a thread that passes through families, regardless of where they move, what language they speak, or how their circumstances change. Rediscovering the family energy and light connects us with our roots.

# The Brownstone

### Ireland

≫ ≪

*Love is the immortal flow of energy that nourishes, extends,*
*and preserves. Its eternal goal is life.*

**Smiley Blanton**

There's an old Gaelic expression that states, "May the roof above you and the hearth before you always be your own." Reflecting upon the history of war-torn Ireland, it is not difficult to understand why a home has been so important to the Irish.

The day was cold, gray, and dreary as I stood outside the wrought-iron gate surrounding the brownstone on West 18 Street, bordering Greenwich Village. At the turn of the century, this modest building meant the world to Maggie O'Connor, an immigrant from County Clare. One of my greatest regrets was that I never had the opportunity to meet dear Maggie, my great-grandmother.

Bursting with optimism, eighteen-year-old Maggie landed at Ellis Island in 1892 with just the clothes on her back and little more than five dollars in her pocket. She wasted no time, however, lamenting what little she had; she secured a position that very afternoon as a cook's helper in a wealthy Park Avenue household.

One year later, she married a fellow Irishman, a handsome longshoreman from Donegal. The two set up housekeeping on the third floor of the brownstone that stood in front of me. Seven years and five babies later, he was tragically killed, crushed between the dock and cargo.

I have often wondered what thoughts must have passed through her mind at that moment. Did she long to return to Ireland? Did she consider putting her children up for adoption? Did she contemplate turning to her priest in the church? I like to fantasize that she squared her narrow little shoulders, jutted her chin forward, and swallowed her fears. The women in our family have always been strong; I like to attribute the origin of that trait to Maggie.

My grandmother remembered little about her father. What she did remember was that shortly after his death, the family moved "downstairs." It seemed that without her husband's income, Maggie could no longer afford the upstairs apartment, and she lost no time in relocating her young family to the basement.

As Maggie herded her children into that damp, dark apartment, she also saved any money she was able to earn. Every morning she carried buckets of coal to the twelve families who lived upstairs. Then, while keeping an eye on her five little ones, she prepared breakfast for the boarders in the large dining area. Her own children would then eat in the kitchen. My grandmother recalled that leftovers had never tasted so delicious.

Several hours each day, Maggie worked as a laundress. The children accompanied her to the various homes of her clients along Seventh Avenue. During the late afternoon, Maggie and the children returned to the brownstone to prepare dinner. As time was a precious commodity, she filled her evening hours taking in "piecework" and sewing by the fire.

Times might have seemed hard, but she never complained. There was always food on the table and a roof over her head. In Ireland, she had neither since famine and poverty were the norm. When I think about Maggie and how hard she worked, I often wish I could have taken her to tea at an elegant hotel, or treated her to a manicure at a spa, but I don't think she would have enjoyed the experience. She probably would have felt nervous, frightened, and even suspicious of such luxurious pampering. She would have felt more comfort escaping to the safety of her basement apartment.

My thoughts had carried me so far away as I stared at the brownstone that I had not noticed the light drizzle had turned into a veritable downpour. As I struggled to open my umbrella, the present owner opened the front door. He seemed kind, gentle, and he smiled shyly as he asked if he could help me.

"I'm sorry," I stammered. "I was admiring your home. I knew someone who used to live here . . . a long time ago." He brightened visibly, and asked if I would like to take a look around inside. He took great pride in the building.

"I'd love to," I responded, climbing the porch steps.

As I walked through the large foyer, dining room, and parlor, I could understand his pride. The home was very special, and had been restored to its Victorian splendor. But I wasn't interested in the main floor. "Could I see the basement?" I asked.

The owner smiled. "That's interesting! That is my favorite part of the house. How did you know?" The stairs were located behind the kitchen, and as I descended, I thought of dear Maggie hauling endless buckets of coal up these very same steps. When I reached the bottom I gasped. Despite the storm howling outside, and the rain beating against the high basement windows, the entire area seemed to be bathed in a light of warmth and love. With overstuffed chairs and ottomans surrounding an open hearth, the room felt like a cozy refuge. But there was more. An inexplicable warm energy permeated the room.

On the mantle was a Greek statue, that I asked about. "It's Hestia, the goddess of home and hearth," the owner answered. "She watches over my home. While I love what she represents, I am not fond of the name Hestia. It seems a bit too formal, don't you think?"

I looked at him with a twinkle in my eye and said, "Would you ever consider renaming her Maggie?" At that moment, quite suddenly, rays of sunlight streamed through the basement windows. The rain had stopped. I felt that Maggie was happy.

***Barbara A. Davey***
*Formerly* "Home Is Where the Hearth Is"

B ringing joy to others can be an experience of sheer delight, especially when done anonymously. Showering gifts on unsuspected children from out of the blue is a delight for everyone—the message truly came from within.

# Candy from Heaven

Germany

≫ ≪

*No person was ever honored for what he received; honor has been the reward for what he gave.*

### Calvin Coolidge

Gail Halvorsen sat on the flight headed for Berlin wondering what "they" would be like. Three years had passed since the end of the war, the war in which every American was taught to hate Germans. In the belly of his airplane, Lieutenant Halvorsen carried a cargo of flour to people who used to be "the enemy." His orders were to supply the people in the Western sector of Berlin with essential supplies. What would it be like? What kind of people were they?

When he arrived at Tempelhof airport, people rushed toward him. "I didn't understand a word they said, but there was so much gratitude and warmth in their eyes. I knew immediately that all I had heard about these people was not true. One day after the relief flights had become commonplace, Lieutenant Halvorsen saw thirty children standing at the airport. They waved to him and called him over to tell him in their broken English how important his flights were to them, "when the weather gets worse, please bring us a little more flour, and we'll be able to manage." Never before had Holversen heard children talk like this. Suddenly he realized what made Berlin so different. All over the world, little ones tugged at his shirtsleeves and begged for candy, but not in Berlin. These children didn't beg for candy because they had never experienced it—they had no idea what candy was. Their main request was for flour.

Gail groped around in his pockets and found two sticks of chewing gum. He broke them in half and gave them to the children. "I thought it would start a fight, but instead the children carefully tore the silver wrapping into little pieces which they distributed among themselves. They even had fun playing with the foil, watching it reflect in the sun."

It was clear to Gail that he had to give the other children something too. The only way was to drop candy outside the fence as he approached the airport. He used gestures to explain his plan to the children. They asked, "How can we tell your plane from all the others?" Gail thought of something he had learned while training for the war, "I'll wiggle my wings," he replied.

With the help of friends and despite severe rationing, Gail managed to scrape together two handfuls of chewing gum, lollipops, and chocolate. He attached these to small parachutes made from knotted handkerchiefs so that they would survive the fall and not injure the children.

Gail spotted the children at the fence from a long way off. When he wiggled the wings of his airplane, the children threw up their arms, jumped into the air, and waved. Gail dropped the parachutes through a hatch before coming in to land. "As I flew back, I saw the children waving parachutes, their little mouths chewing happily. It had worked."

Although scared to death that their superiors might discover and punish them for their unauthorized activity, Gail and his friends continued to organize regular showers of chewing gum over schools and playgrounds. One dull day when he walked into his superior's office at Templehof, he was shocked at what he saw: a large stack of letters all carefully addressed in children's writing to: "Uncle Wiggly Wings, Templehof" and "To the Schokoladen-flieger" (the chocolate flyer). As yet, no one knew who that was.

The following day, however, when the daily newspaper in Berlin showed a photo of Gail's airplane, easily identifiable by its clearly legible number, with little white parachutes dropping to the ground, the game was over. To his surprise and joy, instead of being reprimanded, Gail received enthusiastic praise and permission to continue the "sweet droppings."

Soon thereafter, there were neither enough hankies nor enough cut up pilot shirts to make new parachutes. The children began to send back the pieces of material to be reused while a flood of donations in the form of handkerchiefs and candy began to arrive from the United States.

"It was hard to believe," Gail recalls. Before long, two secretaries were hired to answer all the German children's letters to "Uncle Wiggly Wings."

*Melanie Stunkel*

S ome people never experience love. Others find love in fleeting moments, turn their backs on it, and never find it again. Still others treasure precious moments of deep connection that give the feeling of being fully alive. Peter Kayser shares his story of risk-taking that gave him the validation of his inner knowing.

## Dreams Do Come True

Switzerland

&#8680; &#8678;

*Nunc scio quit sit amor (Now I know what love is).*

### *Virgil*

Marcus, a brilliant computer wizard in his mid-thirties, was trying to sort out his priorities. He had worked as a consultant for many high-tech companies in Switzerland and was well known and respected for his concepts and solutions to complex computer problems.

His main problem was that he worked so hard and long that he had little to no social life. He knew that this was not ideal, so he decided to take a seminar to balance his life. When Marcus came to the seminar he was quite taken with the seminar leader, Lisa. She was good-looking, and she possessed other intangible qualities that made her even more attractive. She was sensitive to people's moods, warm and friendly, and charismatic as well. Marcus studied her during the seminar and found her to be an interesting combination of German precision, focus, and goal-orientation coupled with an Italian fiery temper. Her linguistic skills gave her an international air that made her more intriguing. As he looked at her he assessed that she was a few thousand light years beyond his reach; however, he found her warmhearted, intuitive way of dealing with people irresistible. Marcus completed the seminar and decided to sign up for a second one. He made sure that Lisa would also be leading this one as well.

But after several weeks, Marcus realized that he was falling in love with her. This created a frightening and intense internal conflict. Finally, he chose to use one of the principles in the seminar, "Go for what you want," as a way to approach her, but carefully avoided telling her. He didn't want her to have the slightest discomfort about the intensity of his feelings or his intentions, which he didn't even dare to admit to himself. So he made it a playful game, calling it "Prince and Princess." But how to tell her? A casual social situation might be appropriate.

He asked her to go for a drink after the seminar one evening, and she agreed. They sat in a quiet corner, in a dimly lit bar in Geneva. He ordered champagne cocktails and went into a clichéd conversation about her work, but soon felt an increasing uneasiness. He realized that he could stay in his comfort zone as always, to no avail, or face his fears and let her clearly know that he wanted to spend some social time with her—and get closer to her. But before he could say anything, the music changed and she offered to teach him to waltz. He swallowed his pride, and admitted that his feet didn't always follow his brain, and they started the one, two, three rhythm. After many laughs, and bruised toes, they sat, sipped, and relaxed.

Marcus saw his chance; he took a very deep breath, leaned forward in his chair and said, "I have something to tell you. I want you to give me one weekend of your life." he blurted out. Lisa was shocked. She thought of him as an organized, even a bit conservative person, not exactly a risk-taker in the realms of emotion. Confused, she stuttered "What?" He interjected, "You don't have to answer now. Please don't. It would be a dream to have a woman like you say 'yes' and come away with me for two days together somewhere."

"I hardly know what to say," Lisa mumbled.

"Trust me—and listen" said Marcus, "Here it goes . . . you happen to be my fantasy woman. You are everything I ever dreamed a woman could be. You are beyond my imagination."

"That's very kind of you, Marcus. I am very flattered, but . . ."

"I want to take you away for the weekend to somewhere I've never been before and have always wanted to go. It would be a dream come true for me," Marcus exclaimed.

"Um, uh, er, go away?" Lisa struggled to find words.

"Yes, somewhere magical. It would be an experiment. If you'd say 'yes' it might change my entire perception of life," Marcus explained.

"But, when?"

"After the course is over," replied Marcus.

"What about the sleeping arrangements?" Lisa asked.

"Separate rooms, of course," affirmed Marcus.

"No strings attached?" posed Lisa.

"No strings at all. Just let me spoil you, let me create the illusion that we are smiled upon by fate—an experience I've definitely never had in thirty-five years. My only intention is that we both have a very good time together and I once get a taste of how life could be if it were perfect," declared Marcus.

"I have to think about it," said Lisa. "This all comes as rather a shock, I need some time . . . this is all so sudden," said Lisa. "I must be going now, thank you for the compliment, the drink, the dance, and taking the risk. I will let you know next week about your invitation. Thank you." Then Lisa vanished before Marcus could say a word.

A week went by. Marcus became more and more nervous as each day passed. Finally, Lisa came to him and said, "I would like a word with you." His heart stopped, as he swallowed hard and followed her outside.

"Marcus, I have been thinking about your invitation," Lisa started.

"Let me get this straight. You want to enjoy my company for two days, anywhere I choose, and we will have separate bedrooms, and there are no expectations beyond having a good time together?"

"Exactly!" Marcus replied.

"Look, this isn't something I have ever done before, nor am I exactly at ease with your wish, but why should this be different from anything else. We are clear on the bedroom situation?" Lisa said.

"Clear!" said Marcus.

"Then, I accept!" Lisa said with a slight smile.

Some weeks later Marcus took Lisa to Montreux. They stayed in a lovely hotel right on the beach of Lake Geneva. After having had hours of substantial conversations, framed by an elegant dinner, they decided to have a walk at the seaside. After a while they realized that in a large boat near them there were music and people enjoying themselves.

They decided to enter the boat—and they heard the same music as in the Geneva bar. To Marcus, this seemed like a hint from heaven. He gently took her hand and led her to a large, empty ballroom and started to dance the waltz, self-confident and calm, but ignoring the world around them completely. As he became aware of her engagement and the fact that he created this magic moment, he looked into her eyes, then kissed, and embraced her. After a while, other couples entered the room and joined them dancing; they seemed to understand.

He felt like he was in a trance, in another place. Like a star in the breaking dawn, he became dissolved in a much brighter light.

This completely unexpected outcome, a weekend full of warmth, even bliss, catapulted him into another reality, a reality he never had the chance to experience, in fact never even seriously dared to dream of it. Despite his very sad family history, he was happy, happy as never before in his thirty-five years.

The same way dreaming sleepers are sometimes aware of a reality level above the one they are in, Marcus became aware of another level, a level above normal life, with magical properties, where the rules and beliefs governing his daily life didn't have any significance anymore. Being a lifelong skeptic, he suddenly saw a divine sense of perfection in everything. He left his sarcasm behind and moved on in his life. He no longer thought of himself as someone unable to experience happiness, but realized for the first time that this was clearly an option for him.

*Peter Kayser*

Listening to the whispers of the soul may mean honoring tradition. It may mean celebrating life even when you have very little to celebrate. It may mean reaching out to others who have less than you. Listening to your inner wisdom means being true to your essence while connecting with a higher power of spirit. Mark Dias shares with us why tradition us so important to uplifting the spirit.

# The Festival

Nicaragua

➣ ➢

*On the whole, the happiest people seem to be those who have no particular cause for being happy except that they are so.*

### *William R. Inge*

After nineteen years, we decided to make a return trip to Nicaragua. It was also the first time our children, Jonathan, fourteen, and Raeann, eight, would see the land where their mother grew up. I wanted them to experience part of their culture and to see how these people lived.

My wife had told me about a festival that happens every year on December 7. Over and over again she had told me that I must not miss it. I thought this would not only be a great experience for me but for our children as well.

Several days before the celebration, fireworks and firecrackers were being purchased everywhere. These were not the limited fireworks that you find in cities where fireworks are illegal; these fireworks were real. Throughout the city of Managua, La Purísima, the festival, was the talk of the town. People were preparing their houses for the visitors that would be coming. People were buying trinkets and various types of food to give to the myriad of visitors that would be coming to sing their songs of worship in front of a statue of the Virgin Mary. The traditional foods of La Purísimia, candies, and caramels flooded the markets in preparation.

On December 7, the firecrackers started being set off around 6:00 P.M. After each round of firecrackers, the Nicaraguan sky would light up. For the next six hours sporadic firecrackers and fireworks were heard throughout the streets of Managua. If you didn't know you were witnessing a Nicaraguan tradition that occurs every year at the same time, you might mistake it for a small war.

La Purísima is uniquely a Nicaraguan festival. No other country celebrates this feast day. The firecrackers announce the start of La Purísima and the celebration lasts until midnight. Groups, including adults and children, go from house to house shouting what is known as La Griteria, *¿Quien causa tanta alegría?*" "Who causes so much joy?" And the response, *"La Concepción de María,"* "The Virgin Mary." This is all done in front of altars built by the homeowners. Many of these altars have been in the families for centuries. After La Griteria, the group sings songs to the Virgin Mary from booklets that are purchased for a couple córdobas (the Nicaraguan currency) each. This prompts the residents of the house to distribute the traditional gifts, which include sugar cane, various types of fruit, chicha (a fermented maize drink), toasted maize, and various trinkets.

The economic crisis prompted many to give the visitors basic necessities such as rice, beans, and soap. At the home where we were staying, over nine hundred items were given away. This means there were more than nine hundred people who sang and cheered in front of that altar. I had never seen so many people as I did that night; it was quite a spectacle. Many of the altars were elaborately built and it was also evident there was a lot of money spent on the distributed food and trinkets.

We sat outside as we watched each group approach the bars of the houses. (Many houses in Nicaragua are totally enclosed by bars.) This was not a tradition that was just for the kids. This custom transcended both age and gender. The groups were comprised of individuals of all ages and all shapes and sizes; it was definitely a family event or an event that brought people together. Thousands of people walked up and down the streets visiting each of the various houses. The lady of the house where we were staying, my sister-in-law, would open the barred gates on a group-by-group basis. They would enter, sing their devotionals to the Virgin Mary, and Jonathan and Raeann would grab items from the nine or ten baskets on the patio and distribute them to the group. As each group left the next entered. This scene was repeated over and over again throughout the streets of Managua and continued until midnight.

For one day of the year, Nicaragua was able to escape the reality of its critical economic situation. This quote from Armando Quintero in 1992 sums up the Nicaraguan sentiments during La Purísima. "Neither war nor earthquakes, nor volcanic eruptions, nor acts of terrorism, nor economic difficulties has been able to dampen the fervor of the Nicaraguan people . . . [in their celebration of La Purísima]." The people kept their tradition alive in spite of the economic crisis that impacted the Nicaraguan community.

*Mark Dias*

## YOU WILL FORGET ALL OF THIS AT BIRTH

*You can remember it if you want by unraveling the double helix of inner knowing.*

Remembering and forgetting are the dance of consciousness. If you remembered all the time, there would be no challenge, and if you forgot everything, there would be no game at all. Ultimately, we are one world . . . and we need to remember that we are all human!

# We Are a Nation of . . .

United States

We are a nation of
Many nationalities, many races, many religions—
Bound together by a single unity,
The unity of freedom and equality.
Whoever seeks to set one nationality against another,
Seeks to degrade all nationalities.
Whoever seeks to set one race against another,
Seeks to enslave all races.
Whoever seeks to set one religion against another,
Seeks to destroy all religions.

*Franklin D. Roosevelt*
The Roosevelt Library

Enigma and uncertainty encircle birth and death. We may know when our journey is complete, or we may not, but in either case, each life has its own timeline. Cherish the moments that are precious. Sibylle Alexander shares a mystical story about life cycles.

# Return of the Brother

Ireland

⇒ ⇐

*There is only one terminal dignity—love.*

**Helen Hayes**

Not far from Boyne, Ireland, near the old monastery of Clonard lived a boy named Peter. His mother believed he had been born prematurely, before he was fully developed. Peter thought the angels ran out of time to stitch up his back properly. Each had their way of explaining the hole in his back. The impact on Peter was that he couldn't walk.

Peter was a bright child who brought his parents great joy. His large blue-gray eyes with a dark ring round the iris were memorable. Both his parents were musicians and their friends loved to play for Peter, a child with a deep love of music who was always delighted to listen. Peter's family home was a beautiful old house, with a garden, and a bird paradise that extended to the river.

When Peter's younger brother, Sebastian, was born, Peter was delighted. He rejoiced that his brother was in good health and "whole." It took time until Sebastian grew into a little boy with whom Peter could play. Throughout those early years, first the cradle and then later a cot stood next to Peter's bed or in close proximity to his wheelchair. Sebastian's first memory was of Peter's bright eyes gazing joyfully at him.

One day, Peter had to go to the hospital in Dublin. He grew quite sad and despondent. When asked what was wrong he shook his head, "It's no use telling you, nobody can make my wish come true." Finally he confessed how he longed to hear the birds sing, the rushing sounds of the river, and the wind rustling in the treetops. These were the sounds of home. "If you could play this music to me, then I could imagine I was playing our favorite games in our garden."

From then on his father never went anywhere without a notebook in his pocket. Wherever he went, he stopped and listened to the various birdcalls and wrote down their musical notes. When his father went to see Peter, they played a game. His father would play the notes that the birds had sung, and Peter had to guess which bird belonged to which tune. They both enjoyed this game, and they had great fun together, but something was missing.

One day Peter tentatively asked whether all the melodies could be woven together into one piece of music, just like in nature where all the sounds formed a harmonious melody. Thoughtfully the father walked home along the river busily composing a concert.

Peter's homecoming from the hospital was like a festival. People from all around, neighbors and friends had been invited to welcome him home and play their instruments. Each instrument had been given a solo, and the piano pulled all the various sounds together in a beautiful harmony. Peter's father called it "The Symphony of Nature," to honor his request. Peter and Sebastian were thrilled and requested an encore. Their faces were aglow with delight, which was reward enough for the musicians.

It seemed as if Peter lived with a heightened awareness of everything around him. His frail body recorded each change in the weather as if it was an instrument finely tuned. When sudden storms broke out, Peter was forced to remain indoors. When he heard the call of the wild geese, his father was compelled to scoop him up and carry him out to the fields to watch their flight south. Peter told Sebastian, "Joys and sorrows belong together." But Sebastian did not yet understand his wisdom.

During Lent, Peter's strength seemed to gradually slip away; he lay quietly against his pillow while Sebastian tried ever so hard to cheer him up. He would pick the first spring flowers and scamper in the house, arms outstretched with handfuls for his ailing brother, but nothing seemed to brighten his spirits.

"May I hear the 'Symphony of Nature' once more?" Peter asked his father, and with great effort the musicians assembled the very same evening. When the house was filled with the sounds of nature from his childhood, it was as if summer had just arrived for a visit.

A restless night followed and the doctor was summoned. When he left at dawn Sebastian crept into Peter's sickroom. "Peter," Sebastian began fearfully, "why does Mummy cry in the kitchen?"

"I will tell you if you promise not to cry yourself!" Solemnly Sebastian promised and crossed his heart.

"You know, Sebastian, that when your next birthday comes along you will be eight, then nine, and then ten. I, however, will never ever be more than twelve."

Sebastian looked mystified. "What do you mean? No more birthdays for you?"

Peter searched for an explanation, then his face lit up. "Let me draw a picture for you and then you will understand what I mean."

Sebastian ran to fetch paper and crayons.

"Here is our house with the high roof and the trees next to it . . . behind the Boyne . . . above those clouds . . . But look here . . . there is a hole! Between the clouds, it is all blue, that's the sky. The blue part is an open door. Grown-ups don't understand that I am going to fly through that door into Heaven . . . it may happen quite soon. I had a glimpse of it and I'm really looking forward to going there. So it's silly to cry."

Lowering his voice he whispered, "Sebastian, I have an even bigger secret and you are the only one I trust to keep it. Look at the top left-hand corner of the picture. I'll draw a tiny wild goose, far, far away. Then I'll draw bigger and bigger geese. See how the last and biggest one is now landing on our roof? Well, that's how I'll return. Remember the wild geese. Watch for them."

Sebastian carefully carried the precious picture into his own room to hide it. He was still a bit puzzled, but he felt honored that Peter would confide in him. Time passed, and the inevitable collapse of Peter's frail body came to pass.

When his light coffin was slowly carried to the cemetery, Sebastian searched the sky for the wild geese but none were there. It was not yet time . . .

Long after Sebastian had left home and married a young woman from a northern country, he was looking through some old papers when he discovered Peter's last picture. Recalling his brother's face, he heard his voice saying softly, "That is how I will return. Remember the wild geese. Watch for them!" Quizzical, he placed the picture back into its hiding place.

Sebastian's young wife was expecting her first child. A cradle stood waiting by their bed in their warm comfortable home. One evening, Sebastian was awakened at midnight by his wife pleading, "It's time for the doctor. Fetch him, he has a long way to walk!" Step by step Sebastian had to fight his way against a gale wind that blew against his face. Suddenly he heard a strange sound growing louder and louder until he recognized the cry of the wild geese and the beating of their wings. Flying in strict formation, the flock headed directly toward his home. Then he remembered the "Symphony of Nature," and resuming his walk, he sang it to the wind.

Labor was a long struggle until the young mother gave birth. The cry of the newborn filled the house. When the doctor placed the warm little bundle into the arms of the father, the sight, feel, and touch of the tiny creature overwhelmed him. Sebastian searched for some family features but could find nothing to remind him of anyone. With a soft crooning voice he sang the "Symphony of Nature," and the child stopped crying as if he knew the tune. Inhaling deeply, it slowly opened its tightly closed eyelids and two radiant gray-blue eyes gazed up at Sebastian. These were the eyes of Peter, his lost brother. Now he could share the love once again that had been stored in his heart all these years.

*Sibylle Alexander*

Birth is one of the universal experiences in life. All women who give birth carry their children in their bellies. All mothers pray for a healthy baby. All women who give birth are profoundly grateful for the miraculous gift of life. Witnessing birth is extraordinary in any language. Whether it happens in a hospital, a home, a taxi, or in a mud hut, birth is truly a wonder. Joyce Denton takes us to this moment of truth.

# Birth in Any Language

Nepal

⇒ ⇐

*No joy can equal the joy of serving others.*

**Sai Baba**

After their marriage, Begum accompanied her husband from northern India to western Nepal, in the foothills of the Himalayas. Her husband was a shopkeeper, who traveled frequently to purchase merchandise for his shop. Their trip left her feeling adrift with no connection to this strange land or these new people.

I, myself, was living abroad, in another culture very different from my own. I had recently rented a one-room dehras or "apartment" next to Begum and her husband in the Tansen bazaar (center of town). I had lived in Nepal for eight years, and from time to time experienced home-sickness, especially when the holiday season evoked nostalgic feelings. Those quiet moments when candles and oil lamps flickered from doorways and window ledges, casting streams of light throughout the clear mountain air, brought a deep yearning for a feeling of belonging. Laughter, family reunions, daughters returning home from their husbands' houses dug deep into my soul. It was just the end of October, but every lit candle and platter of brightly colored delicious treats reminded me of the holidays at home.

Begum and I were both foreigners far away from family and friends. Her husband was away again for several days on a purchasing trip. The lights, laughter, and joyousness around us only magnified our loneliness. We sat in silence, comforted by each other's presence.

Laxmi lived with her mother and older sister on the other side of Begum. Laxmi's mother was a nurse, and we often turned to her for minor medical concerns. Begum was pregnant, expecting her first child. As the months passed, the commonality of our feelings formed the foundation of our bond. Even though we didn't spend long periods of time together, there was an unspoken bond that existed between us. The months passed quickly and Begum's baby was due. We talked about the birth and wondered whether her husband would be home at that special moment.

One night, a neighbor daughter's cries awakened me, "Come quickly! Hurry! Begum's baby is coming!" I hurried next door to Begum's dehras. I didn't know what I could do to help, but I did know that I must go there. The neighborhood child assumed, in spite of my denials, that I could deliver babies. I am sure they thought that since I was a foreigner and worked in a hospital that I could handle any medical emergency.

As I entered the room I saw her lying on the floor writhing in pain. I moved forward and sat in the darkness next to Begum's body, lying on a straw pallet on the mud floor. Laxmi had been asked to go for candles, tiny clay oil lamps, and flashlights from a neighbor, anything to provide light since there was no electricity in the dehras; once again, the electricity had been turned off in the bazaar. There we were on the mud floor, in total darkness, with my friend Begum giving birth.

Laxmi returned with one tiny candle stub that gave just enough light to dimly illuminate Begum's form as her labor intensified. Laxmi and her sister looked to me as the person in charge, since their mother, the nurse, was visiting relatives in another village.

All I could think of was the phrase: boil some water. My scanty knowledge of childbirth was gleaned from watching old Westerns on television. I had never delivered a baby, and no matter how I argued about my incompetence, they still looked to me as "the one who knows." I kept begging them to fetch the midwife, Corra.

Begum's delivery was imminent. Begum and the neighbor girls were beseeching me to "Do something!" But I didn't know what to do except watch, wait with them, and try to comfort as best I could. The candle stub was now merely a glimmer, but we saw a dark shadow at the door. At that moment, Corra entered through the low doorway. I thought, thank God, the midwife has arrived!

Corra handed me her flashlight, freeing her hands to help Begum deliver the baby. The weakened beam illuminated only a small ring of light with its center remaining dark. It was no help to a midwife trying to deliver a baby in a now totally dark room. Laxmi was again sent out in the night to the landlord's family to beg for a light, any light. She returned with a flashlight. I switched on the flashlight and saw a tiny dot of light flicker on Corra's sleeve, too small for the needed illumination.

For the remainder of the delivery, I sat on the pallet beside the midwife holding a flashlight in each hand, coordinating the two beams to form one solid patch of light. Moments later, Begum had her baby. There she was, a chubby, robust, and beautiful baby girl.

*"Tato pani! Tato pani!"* Laxmi jumped up from the corner. "What do we do with the hot water?" I didn't know now, since the child was already born, so we never actually used the hot water for the baby.

Quick on my feet, I proposed, "Let's have tea!" We saluted the wonder of life, the midwife's impeccable timing, and God's blessing with this perfect baby. Here we were, two foreigners who found a connection, a loving bond, in this land that was foreign to us both.

In two days Begum asked me to name her baby. I felt honored and suggested the name Anita. I was asked because I held the light when she gave her greatest gift, the gift of life.

*Joyce Denton*

Sharing your life with someone is one of the greatest gifts you can offer. We are all part of the human family. We all deserve to have a home with parents and love. If for some reason we missed the opportunity, we still deserve to receive a second chance. Adoption gives those who lost out on their first option a second chance at the blessings life has to offer. Heather Black lets us celebrate the reunion with an unclaimed family member!

## Adoption Crosses All Borders

Vietnam

⇒ ⇐

*We are all dependent on one another, every soul of us on Earth.*

### *George Bernard Shaw*

Bicycles and motor scooters crisscrossed the busy intersection in downtown Ho Chi Minh City as I wandered through the market stalls shopping for gifts and souvenirs. Halfway around the world from my Colorado Springs home, I cradled my infant daughter, Cecilia, in a shoulder sling as I picked up a tiny wooden statuette and asked the merchant, "How much?"

"Ten dollars," he replied, and like many of the Vietnamese people I encountered, his English was excellent.

The merchant and I were haggling over the price when an elderly woman stepped close and smiled at Cecilia. "She very lucky baby," the woman told me.

I shook my head, my eyes welling with tears. "I'm the lucky one," I insisted, and I still think so, to this very day.

I was in Vietnam to fulfill a promise I'd made fourteen years ago, when I was only twenty-three. Fresh out of college, I'd taken a job as a newspaper reporter with a Boston weekly, and I was thrilled the day my editor sent me on my first overseas assignment.

I was on my way to Bolivia, to cover a local medical team that was correcting birth defects for underprivileged children. The people were humble and poor, but their hearts were full of love. Often twenty-five or thirty cousins, aunts, and uncles would gather to wait with anxious parents while surgeons corrected their child's harelip or other congenital defects.

Then one day I visited a Santa Cruz local orphanage that housed a hundred malnourished little girls dressed in tattered rags. They swarmed around me like bees to nectar, clutching at my hands, my clothes, even my hair. Never in my life had I witnessed such hopelessness and despair.

"These children have nothing—not even someone to love them," I thought, my heart breaking in two. I drew close to me as many of the children as I could, but there were so many, I couldn't possibly comfort them all.

This was just one orphanage in one small town. Around the world I knew there were thousands upon thousands of other abandoned children with no one to fill their bellies or rock them to sleep at night. In a million years I couldn't help them all, but I promised God that one day, when the time was right, I would give an orphan child a home and fill her life with love.

Back in Boston, not a day went by when I didn't think about those children and their sad and hopeless lives. As a young single woman, I wasn't ready to adopt, but twice I visited rural Honduras to work in a clinic and help distribute donated baby supplies.

Eventually I moved home to Colorado, where I met Ralph at a church social. We fell in love, but before I would agree to get married I told Ralph all about my trip to Bolivia and my promise to one day adopt a third-world orphan.

"Your promise is now our promise," Ralph said, and I couldn't have loved him more.

Ralph and I also wanted children of our own, and our hearts filled with joy at the births of our two sons, Karl and Todd, now seven and five. I loved everything about being a mom—changing diapers, teaching my boys to walk and talk, reading them stories at bedtime. Kissing them goodnight, I couldn't help but reflect on how very blessed I was to be able to give my children all the things they needed to grow up happy and strong. But I also remembered all the children who weren't so fortunate, and my sacred promise to God to open my heart and my home to an impoverished orphan.

Last year Ralph and I celebrated our tenth anniversary. Our children were confident, happy little boys, and I knew they'd love to have a baby sister. "I think it's time," I told Ralph, so together we went to Hope's promise, a local agency that specializes in international adoptions.

An agency social worker informed us that our chances of adopting a healthy baby girl would be best in Vietnam. "That would be wonderful," I said, and together Ralph and I waded into an ocean of paperwork and pored through every book we could find about Vietnamese history and culture.

Last April our application was accepted. A few days later the social worker handed me a Polaroid of a precious, dark-haired newborn with a rosebud mouth. "Congratulations, Mom," she said, and for me it was love at first sight.

Her name was Tuyet Lan, but we decided to call her Cecilia, after Ralph's mom. "It will be our way of bringing her into the family," I told everyone, showing them the photo I carried everywhere—especially inside my heart.

But there was still more paperwork to be processed, since both the Vietnamese and U.S. governments had to approve the adoption. Ralph and I lived the next five months in eager anticipation that often turned into impatience. But finally, last September, I flew to Vietnam to meet our new baby girl.

The Tam Binh Orphanage was large and austere. I was welcomed by a tiny, energetic nun named Sister Hai, and my heart pounded as I reached out to accept my precious baby girl.

For the longest time Cecilia gazed up at me with a grim and solemn expression. And then she gave me a big, wide smile. "I already love you so much!" I burst into tears, and for the next six days I hardly put Cecilia down at all.

Unfortunately, there was still a forty-day waiting period before the adoption could be finalized. It was the hardest thing I've ever done in my life, handing Cecilia back to Sister Hai and making the thirty-two-hour trip home alone. "I hope she's still okay," I'd pray every night, but there was no way to find out because communications into and out of Vietnam are so restricted.

I crossed each day off the calendar like an eager child waiting for Santa Claus. Then, finally, the day I'd dreamed about for fourteen years arrived, and I boarded a flight back to Vietnam to bring home our new daughter.

Cradling Cecilia in my arms, I was so enchanted, it was several minutes before I noticed her tiny body was covered with angry welts the size of nickels from scabies, a parasite that thrives in hot, humid climates. A doctor could provide relief, but a whisper of worry filled my heart. Cecilia had been screened for serious diseases, but what if they'd missed something?

"It doesn't matter," I told myself, sweeping away the goblins of doubt. "You're my little girl, and I love you, no matter what."

It was still several days before I would be allowed to take Cecilia home, and we spent the time visiting the Vietnamese countryside and shopping in the local bazaars. I bought a rosewood jewelry box, jade earrings, silk purses and Vietnamese dolls—gifts for each of Cecilia's first eighteen birthdays. I also took rolls and rolls of photos so she'd always know where she came from.

Wherever Cecilia and I went people stopped and smiled at us. It was obvious to all that I was adopting one of their own, and they were thrilled because they knew she was going to have a wonderful life in America.

Sister Hai gave me a Vietnamese outfit for Cecilia's first birthday, and my translator, "Uncle No Problem," gave Cecilia a beautiful ID bracelet engraved with both her new and old names. "Thank you—thank you for everything," I wept when it was time to leave. I hugged everyone in sight, and thirty-two hours later I deplaned in Colorado Springs with twenty-five friends and relatives singing "Cecilia" to welcome us home.

Exhausted, choked with emotion, I handed Cecilia to Ralph. "This is your new daddy," I introduced them, and tears rolled down Ralph's cheeks as he cradled our infant daughter in his arms for the very first time.

Our pediatrician soon gave Cecilia a perfect bill of health, and today, at eleven months, she's a perpetual motion machine—chasing her brothers around the house and playing with our dog, Pal. Karl and Todd dote on their little sister, bringing her toys and fighting over whose turn it is to play with her. And every evening when Ralph comes home from work, Cecilia screams with delight when he lifts her high in the air and asks, "Who's my sweet baby girl?"

Rocking Cecilia to sleep after yet another busy day, I see again in my mind the blue metal bars of the orphanage crib. I hear the question I'm asked by so many people—"Why did you choose to adopt a baby from Vietnam?"—and my answer is always the same: To have a daughter to love. To give a child a family. To fulfill my promise to God.

Watching Cecilia's peaceful face, I breathe a prayer of thanks.

*Heather Black*

Through history, the human species has made incredible advances in transportation, medicine, communication, technology, and modern conveniences. The one area in which we appear to be the most primitive is in our human relations. Our biggest challenge and opportunity is in learning to live in harmony with each other. It is in the area of human consciousness evolution that we, as a species, have the most to learn. The new frontier is not in space or the depths of the ocean, but rather in the human spirit, heart, and will. The opportunity is clear, the challenge has been presented—the choice is up to each of us. Can we consider the possibility of living in peace with our fellow humans?

## One World, One Heart

United States

≫ ≪

*This is still a world in which too many of the wrong things happen some-where. But this is a world in which we now have the means to make a great many more of the right things happen everywhere.*

**Margaret Mead**

We all hear the same sounds. We look up and see the same sky. We cry the same tears. Our feelings and emotions are the same. All mothers are sisters. All fathers are brothers. All children are one.

Yet there is hate. There is violence. There is intolerance. There is confusion among people. We don't try hard enough to understand each other. We don't seem to realize that we all have the same basic needs, no matter who we are or what part of the world we come from.

We must understand the differences among us and celebrate the sameness. We must make the world a place where love and friendship dominate our hearts. Equality, respect, compassion, and kindness must guide our actions. Only then will we be able to peacefully and lovingly live the life we each choose.

*Susan Polis Schutz*

# For Those in Search of Meaning

*The Rules for Being Human are universal truths that exist in every culture, every race, every religion, and in both genders. They give context and relevance to the human experience. They connect us to our humanity and make the journey meaningful. They unite us as one! It takes the personal commitment of each person to make the difference.*
*Start today! You matter!*

### Chérie Carter-Scott, Ph.D.

# Contributor Biographies

*Dr. Ichak Adizes* is a world-renowned author and consultant to top management and heads of state. His seven books have been translated into twenty-two languages. He was a professor at UCLA Anderson School of Management and Recanti School of Business, Tel Aviv University. The documentary about the event described in his story is available from Adizes@adizes.com.

Shoham Adizes
Adizes Institute
2815 East Valley Road,
Santa Barbara, CA 93108
Phone: (805) 565-2901, ext. 107
Fax: (805) 565-0741
E-mail: Shoham@adizes.com
Web site: www.adizes.com

*Eri Adrian* received his bachelor of science in electrical engineering in 1994. He works for an IT company in Jakarta, Indonesia. Eri enjoys swimming, tennis, singing, playing piano, and writing in his spare time. He plans to compile all his writings into a book.

Web site: www.e-drian.com

*Shubhra Agrawal* a social activist working toward women's empowerment by creating avenues of economic independence and supporting entrepreneurship. Through networking and constant interaction, she engages women's groups in social development and home businesses. She travels extensively in northern India interfacing with various NGOs, educational institutes, and the creative world of artists, etc.

Shubhra Agrawal
B-382 New Friends Colony
New Delhi, India
Phone: 6830437
Fax: 6429529
E-mail: vashusugar@bol.net.in

*Mollie Ahlstrand* was born and raised in northern Ethiopia, in the Tigre province, in a family of five brothers and three sisters; her father was a local food merchant. Mollie came to Santa Barbara at the age of twenty-six, and has lived here and in Italy ever since. For about five years she worked in some of the most famous restaurants in Italy, in such cities as Bologna, Padova, Rome, and Orvietto. She apprenticed under the famous Italian chef Gianfranco Vissani, and she was a pasta chef in Rome at a restaurant named Arturo's Aurelia Antica. The owners have come to Santa Barbara to visit with Mollie just recently.

Mollie has pursued her career as a chef specializing in the cuisine of northern Italy with vigor, and she hopes everyone will appreciate the value of fresh food prepared by hand in the old classical method. After working for several years in Italy, she and her husband, who commuted from Santa Barbara to Italy on a regular basis, decided that it was time to open her own restaurant.

For the past seven years, at her Trattoria Mollie, located at 1250 Coast Village Road, Montecito, Mollie has served guests from all over this country and Europe. "Fresh food prepared by hand" is the guiding principle for Mollie's offerings, and she purchases many of her vegetables at the farmer's markets, and several of her seafood items are delivered fresh daily directly by Santa Barbara fisherman.

*Diana Gloria Alegre-Pestano* received her bachelor of science in nursing and her master of arts in nursing from the University of the Philippines Manila in 1993 and 1999. She teaches nursing students in the same university. Diana enjoys writing poems and short stories, traveling, and studying different cultures.

E-mail: dgpestano@hotmail.com

*Sibylle Alexander,* born in 1925 in Hamburg, Germany, studied literature and theology. She worked for Radio Hamburg and Radio Scotland and moved to Edinburgh in 1955, where she researched Celtic Christianity and published four collections of Celtic stories, including *Told by the Peat Fire,* in 1999. She is a member of the International Storytelling Club, Netherbow, Edinburgh, and has five children and twelve grandchildren.

Sibylle Alexander
Galashiels
TD 1 2AU
Scotland, UK

*Errol Broome* lives in Melbourne, Australia, and divides her time between her family, the garden, and writing. A former journalist, she now concentrates on writing for children. Her books have been published in Australia and the United States and translated into many languages.

Errol Broome
33 Seymour Grove
Brighton Beach
Victoria 3186
Australia

*Jan Burnes* is director and founder of a consultancy firm specializing in providing training in sales, customer service, and communication skills. Previously the director of a top performing company employing over one thousand people, Jan now consults for many of the top Fortune 500 companies, training people at all levels to achieve higher standards of performance.

E-mail: jburnes@businessinaction.com.au.

*Anne Colledge,* educated at Homerton College, Cambridge, taught deaf children for thirty years. *Northern Lights,* her children's book with a deaf hero, explores deafness in exciting stories set in beautiful northeast England. Read the true story about Freddie the dolphin. Anne has five grandchildren, kayaks, swims, and cycles.

E-mail: Anne.Colledge@btinternet.com
Web site: www.annecol.co.uk

*Linda Coverdale* was born Canadian and in her long career as a travel agent traveled to many different countries. Her travels included eight months on a sailboat traveling down the U.S. Intra-Coastal Waterway and the Bahamas. She is now retired and lives with her husband in California.

*Pamela Harman Daugavietis,* author of *Women's Voices, Women's Visions,* is a writer for the DeVos Children's Hospital Foundation and the Blodgett Butterworth Health Care Foundation in Grand Rapids, Michigan. She conducts journaling workshops throughout the Midwest and is a graduate of the Ohio State University School of Journalism.

E-mail: phd@iserv.net

*Gunter David* was a reporter on major newspapers for twenty-five years and a Pulitzer Prize nominee, before obtaining a master's degree in family therapy. Retired from Johnson & Johnson, where he counseled employees and their families, he has had fifteen stories published in literary journals and anthologies in recent years.

*Barbara Davey* is an executive director at Christ Hospital in Jersey City, New Jersey, where she is responsible for public relations and fundraising. She holds bachelor's and master's degrees in English from Seton Hall University. A program near to her heart is "Look Good, Feel Better," a service that provides complimentary wigs to women undergoing treatment for cancer. She and her husband, Reinhold Becker, live in Verona, New Jersey.

E-mail: wisewords2@aol.com

*Joyce Denton* graduated from the University of Kansas with a degree in physical therapy, lived eight years in Nepal as a medical missionary, and currently lives with her husband atop a beautiful Arkansas mountain. She has authored a book of prose, *Heart to Heart,* and been published in the *Nepal Medical Journal.*

E-mail: jbaldwindenton@yahoo.com

*Mark Dias* received his bachelor's degree in accounting from San Jose State, and his MBA from Golden Gate University. He speaks Spanish and is very interested in the Hispanic culture. He is American and his wife is Nicaraguan. They were married in Managua, Nicaragua, two years before the Sandinista revolution. Mark's father-in-law was a senator in Nicaragua during the Somoza Regime. Most of his wife's family is currently living in the United States as a direct result of the Sandinista revolution.

E-mail: mark24609@aol.com

*Francesco Garripoli* is an author, television producer, and Qigong practitioner and wellness advocate. His documentary, *Qigong: Ancient Chinese Healing for the 21st Century,* airs on PBS-TV, and with his wife, Daisy, he teaches workshops worldwide. Videos, books, the free *Breathe Deep* newsletter, and study trips to China are available.

E-mail: Francseco@wuijiproductions.com
Web site: www.wujiproductions.com

*Blair P. Grubb, M.D.,* is a professor of medicine and pediatrics at the Medical College of Ohio, where he is director of the Cardiac Electrophysiology and Pacemaker Laboratory. A native of Baltimore, Maryland, he has published over 150 scientific papers. In addition, he publishes essays and poetry. He is married and the father of a daughter and a son.

*Gabrielle Haubner* received her teaching diploma from the Academy of Paedagogics of Salzburg in 1984. She resigned from her job at the airline on May 17, 2002, and started her own sales and marketing company in July 2002.

Web site: www.hyomarketing.com

*Lee Hill-Nelson* has always been a Texan, except for twenty months' service in the U.S. Navy WAVES. She is a retired church secretary, mom, wife, and grandma, and freelance writer, and mentors teenage boys in reading at a youth center.

Lee Hill-Nelson
2341 Lake Ridge Circle
Waco, TX 76710
E-mail: LCountrymiss@aol.com

*Lois Logan Horn* received her bachelor of arts degree with high honors from the University of Washington in 1944 and a masters of social work degree at the University of Washington in 1952. She was a school social worker with Seattle schools for twenty years.

E-mail: 1horn2@mindspring.com

*David Irvine* is an internationally known speaker, workshop leader, author of *Simple Living in a Complex World: Balancing Life's Achievements,* and coauthor of *Accountability: Getting a Grip on Results.* He lives in the foothills of the Rockies with his wife and daughters.

Web site: www.davidirvine.com

*Phyllis Johnson* writes grant proposals, legislation, magazine and news articles, technical manuals, and anything else that needs to be written. She has been a lobbyist, public relations director, counselor, program analyst, EMT, and elephant-sitter. She coexists with several intelligent companions, including her husband and cats.

E-mail: Pendragonetc@prodigy.net

*Amisha Kanoria* received her bachelor of arts in 1986. She enjoys traveling, reading, writing, and computers. She has published articles and poems in Indian magazines, and also plans to write for other newspapers and magazines.

*Charles Kastner* earned an undergraduate degree from Whitman College in 1977. He holds advanced degrees in three disciplines and has written on diverse subjects ranging from biotechnology to reviews of exotic marathons. He is currently working on a book about the history of ultra-marathoning.

E-mail: bak@nwlink.com

*Bernard Lernout* received his master's degree in computer science from the University of Gent, Belgium, in 1974. He is now a freelance market validation expert and teaches accelerated learning skills. Having raised five daughters, he and his wife, Agnes, are now fulfilling a life dream: a Retreat Center for Integral Lifelong Learning.

Web site: www.claritywell.com

*Maria Tereza Maldonado, MA,* is a clinical psychologist and member of the American Family Therapy Academy. She has published twenty-five books, works as a lecturer, and volunteers in social projects. She lives in Rio de Janeiro.

E-mail: mtmaldonado@usa.net
Web site: www.mtmaldonado.com.br

*Dr. William T. (Ted) Moore* is the Belinberg Professor of Finance at the University of South Carolina's Moore School of Business. He also serves as editor of the *Journal of Financial Research,* a periodical devoted to scholarly studies in financial economics, and is author of *Real Options & Option-Embedded Securities,* published by John Wiley & Sons, 2001. Dr. Moore served as a U.S. Army infantryman in Vietnam from 1968 to 1969.

*L. Alberto Py, M.D.,* is a psychoanalyst in Rio de Janeiro. He writes a Sunday column in the newspaper *O Dia* and has published five books about health and self-help and also about group psychotherapy. He travels around Brazil lecturing on the quality of life. He has five sons, thirty-three years to eighteen months, four granddaughters, and two grandsons, for the moment.

E-mail: lpy@pobox.com

*Janine Sheperd* received her bachelor of arts diploma in education (physical education) from the University of Technology in Sydney, Australia, in 1992. She is a commercial pilot and aerobatic flying instructor as well as being an author and motivational speaker. Janine is married and has three children. She enjoys horse riding, swimming, and being with her children.

E-mail: janinesheperd@ozemail.com.au

*Joanna Campbell Slan* is one of the most frequent contributors to the Chicken Soup for the Soul series. She is the author of five books on scrapbooking as well as the motivational book *I'm Too Blessed to Be Depressed.* A motivational speaker, Joanna has spoken all over the world on the importance of family stories.

E-mail: savetales@aol.com

*Lilia Reyes Spindola* is a Mexican writer who writes about values and conscience. She also writes children's stories. She had the privilege of meeting Mother Teresa of Calcutta, and this close experience changed her life, making her realize that we can serve the world and each other with love in everything we do. "We all can change the world."

*Astrid Stahlberg,* art therapist, author, and consultant, has run her own development business since 1981. Her career is international, having worked in an American consulting business, in hospital administration in the Congo, and as a deacon in Switzerland. She ran a private prison on a cargo ship in the Baltic Sea for seven years.

Astrid Stahlberg
SE 167 41 Bromma-Stockholm
Porfyrvaegen 9, Sweden
Phone: 46.8.26 76 06
E-mail: astrid@astridstahlberg.se
Web site: www.astridstahlberg.se

*Bob R. Steevensz* is a life coach. His coaching firm is called Life Design Consultancy.

Bob R. Steevensz
Bertrand Russellstraat 18
Amsterdam the Netherlands
Phone: 011-3120-6231965
Fax: 011-3120-4635322
E-mail: b.steevensz@chello.nl

*David Taub* was born in England, but is a U.S. resident who is extensively published in *Lecturer.* He is a member of the National Union of Journalists and the Florida Writers' Association. His coauthored book, *Language of the Souls,* was an entrant for the 2001 Pulitzer for Letters.

*Jan Toncar* was born in Czechoslovakia in 1919. After secondary education, he went to an art school. Germans occupied his country. He was a scout who joined the resistance movement that sent people via safe routes to Poland and later to Hungary via Slovakia. Those who reached Yugoslavia had to join the French Foreign Legion to be able to reach Syria and France. In France, they joined the Czechoslovak Army. After brief training, they were sent to the front. After France made peace with Germany, they made their way south to Sete and took an Egyptian cargo boat to Gibraltar and England, where they camped on the grounds of Lord Cholmondeley. In 1944, they were sent to France as far as Dunkirk, where they were taken and transferred into the U.S. Army and went to Czechoslovakia. After the war, he wrote his memoirs, which should have been published in 1948 but were stopped by the communists. It took him a year to get himself and his English wife out of Czechoslovakia.

*Giselle Tonee* is a skilled spiritual life strategist and healer. She passionately guides individuals (humans and animals of all ages) and groups toward self-healing and acceptance of their divine gifts. Professional qualifications in education and counseling and a masters of business complement her intuition.

*Desmond Tutu,* recipient of the Nobel Peace Prize in 1984, served as Archbishop of Cape Town, South Africa, from 1986 until 1996. In

1995, Archbishop Tutu was appointed Chairman of the Truth and Reconciliation Commission. He continues to play an important role worldwide as a spokesperson for atonement and forgiveness.

*Jane C. Willhite* is cofounder of PSI World, a nonprofit educational corporation. She and her late husband, Thomas, founded PSI World in 1973. Mrs. Willhite is also president of PSI Seminars, which presents a variety of seminars on communication, self-concept, and leadership. Individuals in both the general public and business communities learn techniques and tools for gaining more control, freedom, power, and happiness in their lives. PSI is an organization dedicated to the belief that we all possess power and strengths that remain virtually untapped throughout our lives. These potentials, as well as a greater joy and aliveness, can be made available to everyone through comprehensive educational programs. Jane has proven herself to be a gifted motivational speaker, appearing before thousands to share her deep insights of human nature, her personal experience, and her vast knowledge of the human potential movement. Jane is committed to making a positive difference in this world and to striving for world peace, a dream she hopes will become a reality in her lifetime.

*Dr. Michelle Woodhouse* was born in San Mateo, California. She took her undergraduate degree at Mount Holyoke College in Massachusetts, a masters in religion and a masters in sacred theology at the Lutheran Theological School in Philadelphia, Pennsylvania. She completed her doctorate in pastoral care and counseling at the School of Theology, Claremont, California. She was ordained deacon in 1985 and priest in 1986 by Bishop John Coburn of Massachusetts. For the past ten years, she has served as the associate rector at All Saints Church with special responsibility for pastoral care, the Seniors' Program, the Outreach Program, and Health Ministries. Michelle is passionate about developing a vision and making it come true with the help of members of the parish, working to meet the needs of the parish and community according to the particularities of persons and place. She is also passionate about her alpaca ranch!

*Christine Wotowiec* has a degree in social work and is a certified horticultural therapist and master gardener, and established a horticultural therapy program within the school system where she was employed. After raising their children, she and her husband moved to Tennessee.

Phone: (423) 533-2732

*Razzan Zahra* is an English graduate student at Sonoma State University in northern California, where he has taught a class in Modern Standard Arabic and one on Middle Eastern Women in Muslim Society. He enjoys doing weight training, aerobics, and swimming. Once he graduates, he hopes to obtain a Ph.D. in education and cultural studies.

E-mail: razzanzahra@pon.net

*Meguido Zola* is a teacher and university professor and, by vocation, a traveling storyteller, poet, and award-winning writer for children and young adults. Meguido teaches workshops in storytelling, spirituality, and travel as pilgrimage.

Meguido Zola
Faculty of Education
Simon Fraser University
Burnaby, British Columbia,
Canada V5A 1S6
E-mail: zola@sfu.ca

Dear Reader,

This year marks the thirtieth year that my organization, The MMS Institute, has been supporting people in making their dreams come true. I started the organization in October 1974, expanding internationally in 1988, and worldwide in 1998.

We have received numerous requests from people around the world who have read one or more of my ten books and would like to either represent MMS or conduct MMS workshops, seminars, and trainings in their local areas. These people are from countries around the world.

Since it has always been our purpose to support people in having what they want, we are offering licensing opportunities to enable and empower you to do the MMS work where you live. There are six licensing options with thirty-four courses, from trainer independent to trainer dependent, including train the trainer and on the job training. These liscenses are for like-spirited, like-hearted, and like-minded men and women who have the strong "message" to do this work either part-time, full-time, as an avocation, or as a profession. Seminars are based on the Game Rules series of books, Negaholics Programs, Personal Development Courses, Corporate Programs, Professional Training, and Corporate Processes.

If you've ever dreamed of having your own business (or adding these programs to your repertoire) and building it around the theme of supporting people in making their visions, dreams, and goals become reality, this is the time to consider making *that dream* come true.

We will be offering this opportunity to coaches, trainers, consultants, entrepreneurs, therapists, ministers, and retirees who want to make an even bigger difference

If you know people who might be interested feel free to pass the word so that they can inquire further.

This is an exciting milepost in MMS history. Throughout these past three decades we started in San Francisco in 1974, grew nationally in the '70s and '80s, expanded internationally in 1988, had our *New York Times* number one best-seller in 1998 published in thirty-six countries, grown in media exposure and name recognition, and now in 2004 we are empowering others in living the dream and passing on the torch.

MMS stands for respect, dignity, and fulfilling all of your dreams. Let's make it possible for everyone everywhere to experience this!

***Chérie Carter-Scott, Ph.D.***
Founder

# About the Author

*New York Times* number one best-selling author Chérie Carter-Scott, Ph.D., has been coaching change successfully since 1974. Dr. Carter-Scott is an international author, entrepreneur, consultant, lecturer, teacher/trainer, coach, and seminar leader. Her company has reached millions of people worldwide. Some of Dr. Carter-Scott's Fortune 500 corporate clients are AMI, FMC, American Express, IBM, GTE, State Farm Insurance, Burger King, and *Better Homes and Gardens* magazine.

In 1974, Dr. Carter-Scott founded the MMS Institute, Inc. (the Motivation Management Service Institute), which specializes in personal growth training programs and workshops, corporate consulting, and customized training programs worldwide. For the past thirty years she and her partner and sister, Lynn Stewart, have empowered thousands of individuals to redesign their lives personally and professionally. By way of their unique and inspired work, they continue to help others in initiating life-changing choices.

To learn more you may contact:

Dr. Chérie Carter-Scott
P.O. Box 30052
Santa Barbara, CA 93105
The MMS Institute: (800) 321-6342 in the U.S.
In California: (805) 892-4440
International: 001 805 892-4440
Fax: 001 805 892-4410

E-mail: info@themms.com
Web sites: www.TheMMS.com and www.drcherie.com

Dr. Carter-Scott lives with her husband in Nevada. She divides her time between her office in Santa Barbara and her international interests in Europe, Asia, and Africa.